By Design

ISBN-13: 978-0-9994538-0-3
ISBN-10: 0-9994538-0-7
First Printing January 2018

Front Cover design by Marcia Lewis
Back Cover design by ThomasMax (Lee Clevenger & R. Preston Ward).

Published by: Divacity Press, a ThomasMax Company

ThomasMax Publishing
P.O. Box 250054
Atlanta, GA 30325
404-799-1144/404-368-3997
www.thomasmax.com

By Design

Marcia Lewis

Divacity Press/ThomasMax

FOREWORD

Everything that is being said in this body of work has already been said. At the designated time, there is a way in which something is said that can pierce the very fiber of ones being, it also resonates in the spirit. This doesn't usually happen the first time one might hear something. Over the years there have been certain aphorisms and metaphors that I've stored in my mind, that have been repeated throughout my lifetime in so many ways. One bright day, these fanciful little expressions, that I paid very little attention to in the past, have shed a bright light in a strikingly different way. All the while, adding a completely new dimension to my world. Maybe people call it enlightenment. That moment when you truly get it, whatever that might be. So, as we journey through certain aspects of my life, I humbly ask you to keep an open mind, relax and enjoy the ride.

The purpose of this book is to share with you meaningful life lessons I've encountered. There are lessons that have propelled me to a deeper spiritual path. I consider it a privilege to be able to record some of these accounts because many are not here to do so. I recall my first College Professor say, on the first day of class, that a large percentage of us (something like 95% which I thought was a bit over the top) would be in the insane asylum, an alcoholic or dead. She said it with such confidence it actually shocked me as it did everyone in attendance. Even though 95% was a high ratio, she might have been using it as a bit of a scare tactic, there was some truth to her statement. As it stands today, many of my loved ones have passed along the highway of life and gained some other dimension. That dimension is yet to be known to me; it is still a mystery to any of us still living. I guess I haven't made it quite that far yet. As long as I keep living, I am sure to catch up. I've been told often times that I had better make good use of the time I have left for we know not the day nor the hour . . .

My desire is to speak into the lives of those who will take the time to read, to listen and be touched in a way that rings a bell or two inside your soul in a personal way. May this book bring life, resonate and awaken the power from within. If nothing else, I should only hope that this will be fulfilling in some small way. I hope it will be an interesting piece that journeys into the quiet spaces. Although I do not consider myself an overtly religious person, I am a very private spiritual person. There are basic Bible principles to follow and to learn from. I am not one to quote a lot of scripture to you and I am far from someone who professes to tell you every story in the book, but I have studied and I believe that I have collected some valuable empowerment tools that I can impart to others. I will say that the number One verse that has always stood out in my mind is found in Philippians that says, "I can do all things through Christ who strengthens me." Why you ask? I know this to be true because I have tried Him and He has proven over and over and again and again. Every day, I see the miracle of the Lord and His majestic handy work in my life. All of these lessons are a reflection of God in every way.

It's when you've heard THE VOICE a million times and it meant close to nothing. Like a beautiful little flower bud looking dormant as it quietly sits there, awaiting its divinely appointed time to bloom while absorbing all its vital nutrients. One fine, fine day the meaning of life blossoms into the most pleasant, aromatic, vibrant colored flower; as fragrant as a lovely day at seaside.

It is with humility and great honor that I present little pieces of me as a gift from Him through me to you.

THANK YOU

I would never begin a project of any sort without giving thanks where it is due. I am grateful to so many loved ones that I cannot begin to name all without overlooking some.

Master of the Universe, god Almighty, Allah, Jehovah, Yahweh, Adonai, Prince of Peace, Elohim. It matters not what you call Him, but that you do call Him. He is the reason I exist and the one who gives me the strength to move forward, even when I find myself complacent. The way in which things are designed, I am convinced that things do not happen simply by coincidence. There is a Master Designer, that might be called by many different names, but He is the only source who could begin to orchestrate such perfection. Everyone has these stories yet it is the way in which they are delivered that makes a difference. No human could begin to oversee things as the Master does. It is pleasing to be able to chronicle some of these things as they unfold and then proceed to share them with you. That is a gift within itself and with thanksgiving, it brings great pleasure to share some of these stories with the audience. Thus, here are just a few.

To Robbie and Fred Lewis, my dear parents who have taken me by the hand and gingerly guided me through this path called life and educated me about the important things in life, so that I might find my way. My mothers' sisters, my dear Aunts, may their souls rest in peace. They took great time to help guide and direct me in my days of youth. To my sons who have trusted me to lead, guide and direct their lives. With you two I find balance, love, harmony and stamina. To my Princes', my rocks of whom I am most proud to be called Mom.

My family and friends have been tremendous with an out pouring of encouragement and love. Without them I would not be able to take this courageous step today. To great teachers everywhere; I have a great respect for those who serve humanity in this capacity. I don't mean the ones that are in the teaching profession specifically, but to those who truly wish to serve human kind for the greater good in this world through the precious art of teaching in every capacity. Music has been a teacher, a healer, a soother and next to God and family, there is nothing greater for me. All kinds of music genres have inspired me over the years. I am ever grateful for the contributors of the art form (music, visual, literary, screen, theatre, etc.), that have gone before us and those still here. To Mr. Shearwood Fleming and all the unsung heroes, we are grateful for your generous contributions. To a plethora of artists, civil rights leaders, philosophers, orators and ancestors, I thank all of you. Dr. Angelou, your love always transcended and moved me in a way that inspired me to higher heights in literature. You were most influential as you so eloquently exuded love through writing. The inner-weaving of my Mom's presence will grace the fabric of this work. Mom, I love you! This one's for you. I know in your resting place you are smiling down.

Once again, to all my loved ones, family and friends let me publicly acknowledge how wonderful it is to have you in my life. Thank you for loving me just the way I am.

This book is dedicated to the memory of my precious Mom. The inner-weaving of her presence will grace the fabric of this work.

TABLE OF CONTENTS

CHAPTER ONE

POETRY IN MUSIC MOTION

Along life's journey, I've learned to pay attention. Life will tell you something if you listen attentively. The key is to tune in when life nudges us in a certain way that beckons our attention enough to acknowledge, to process and digest the meaning. It is easier said than done. The sooner it is done, the better. Take it from a professional who has ignored these little tugs for much too long. I guess with maturity comes a time to rise, listen and factor in. Then and only then are we able to carry the torch. Dr. Maya Angelou said it best in her poem, 'Still I rise'. We must rise as we grow and mature; it is a mandate. Real life begins for me at a new place as I gracefully tread into my 50s. This is the second half of my life and it is necessary to make it count, hence, tackling my bucket list. One project is this book which has been in the making since High School days. (Even though, at the time I had no idea). Thanks to dear Mrs. Payne, my English teacher who discovered my writing ability. I was so terribly shy in high school, but I loved English. English literature and music combined together was part of Mrs. Payne's teaching strategy. She was a small framed woman, with long, scraggly hair who always reminded me of a Janis Joplin type character. Mrs. Payne wore many necklaces adorned by ivory pendants. She wore strong vanilla and patchouli perfumes, so much so that you could smell her before you saw her. With a boisterous laugh, she was bold and loud. Mrs. Payne had no problem with telling students exactly where to get off if one dared to disturb her groove in class. It was always a groove with her. What a character she was. Mrs. Payne taught me what a real live "hippie" was like as she exposed me to the musical poetry of Gil Scott Heron. Her favorite recording was "The Revolution will not be televised." Due to my quiet nature, usually well-mannered and courteous disposition, only speaking when spoken to, I thought for sure I would go unnoticed. How wrong was I? It was the exact opposite. I could tell she was intrigued by my work which was very flattering. Mrs. Payne's mode of operation was such that she would stand over my shoulder ever so discreetly and read the material. She only did this a few times before she would read them to the class almost without my consent. Seeing that I was a little uncomfortable being exposed, she would read it silently then audibly ask out loud, so the entire class could hear, "Can I read your work to the class?" By that time, she'd placed me at the center of the classes' attention. After being thoroughly embarrassed, I would oblige. I don't think she would have taken no for an answer anyway. I would surrender so that I did not draw any more attention to myself than necessary. I became the prime example in her class and she would consistently call me to either read my work to the class or she would read it herself. She encouraged me to look up and over the book or pen and paper long enough to realize people were listening and sometimes interested. She forced me out of my shell, which made me very uncomfortable at the time but today, I am forever grateful. I wish I could tell her what an impact she made in my life, but I am sure she is probably no longer with us as she was probably well into her 40s or 50s then. I could no longer hide it under a bushel. My writing blossomed under the tutelage of a one of a kind, wonderfully original woman who was a walking work of art. Although misunderstood by many, Mrs. Payne was a celebrity on campus in her own right.

Around the same time, I was introduced to yoga and Ayurveda practices. Though I never confirmed it, Mrs. Payne seemed to constitute this kind of a karmic lifestyle. These practices enhanced my thinking process and opened my mind to a much broader perspective as I found intrigue in the many wonders and mysteries of the world. High school is typically the time to experiment and I was no different. This influenced my writing and the overall quality of my life as a young teen. As I learned more about myself, world religion with an emphasis on the Eastern philosophies, helped me begin to develop my inner-thoughts. It opened a portal that helped me to reach my "higher" self through practice. This place of solace was remarkable; I could be quiet and reflective while reading and writing. I read many books having to do with Tibetan religion, their cultures and practices. I found this work fascinating. World culture, language, customs, music, religion, cuisine and lifestyle were things that were of interest on my quest for a deeper knowledge and understanding of my inner self. It was amazing to learn about other countries and their lifestyles. The thought of the world at my fingertips was fascinating. Studying the ways of life in other parts of the world gave me a profound understanding of other peoples' customs which reach beyond invisible barriers that are unnecessarily in place. I found myself in a very comfortable place knowing so many things that I didn't know. In fact, Earth, Wind & Fire was the first group that I knew practiced a lot of ancient world religion and philosophy. This was a perfect space for me to be in at the time. It opened my mind to spiritual reality and all that it had to offer.

My Mom exposed me at a prime age to the arts of all kinds. This exposure which included musical theatre of all kinds, dance ensembles, such as Geoffrey Ballet, Alvin Ailey Dancers and The Dance Theatre of Harlem, led me to the lifelong love affair with the arts. At the same token, we attended many concerts and art festivals. She wanted me to have a sense of all the arts; literature, visual art and all types of music. The wonderful singers were most fascinating and we saw the best of the best. She took me to see Ella Fitzgerald, Sarah Vaughn, Joe Williams, Nancy Wilson and many more. She loved Nancy Wilson and would listen to her music frequently. I can recall a time when we were driving in the car and Mom was humming a tune and it was so sweet to me that I can hear her voice today just humming along, as if it were yesterday. I told her that very day that she sounded like Nancy Wilson and she never forgot it. I think she was really touched by my saying so, but she honestly was my Nancy Wilson in real life in so many ways; she sounded so beautiful to me. Mom had a voice of an angel. Her elegance, her charm, her wit, even her sassy sarcasm she could interpret through her voice. It was one of the many special moments we shared.

I wanted to pattern myself after her in most every way. I was beginning to emulate those things a bit more when I was about 16 as I blossomed into a young woman. The poetry, the reading, the world culture and music sent me on quite a journey for such a young person. The idea that infinite possibilities were achievable through various theologies and practices including my Christianity made the world a wondrous place. As I prepared to graduate earlier than most everyone in school due to a couple of grades skipped, I heard about the Julliard School of Music. This is the school I aspired to attend. Although, we were unable to afford it, no one would stop me from dreaming. I have always had a vivid imagination so it was nothing for me to begin to create my own Julliard in my mind. I believed at the time that going to Julliard would be my ticket into the entertainment world on a professional level. I was so wrong. I later learned I didn't really need it. I didn't know at the time how infinite possibilities would show up in my life but I believed they would. I suppose I could say that even though I never made it to Julliard, in many ways, Julliard came to me.

My very first concert was the Jackson 5 — the opening act for James Brown. I cannot remember who I went with but I don't think it was with my parents. I was so mesmerized by the stage and what it represented to me; I could have been with King Kong and forgotten. It was a game changer for me right then and I've never been the same since. It was a majestic experience and I knew I had to surround myself in lights one way or another. Of course, there were many things I had questions about. I had no idea how, but I knew I wanted it and I would always envision myself on stage with them.

I have always been on this quest to feed my spirit with things that amaze me. Mom used to tell me stories about the times when I was a tiny tot. I'd be in a room quietly entertaining myself where she could have an eye on me, while she tended to chores. She would look around to check on me and find it far too quiet; I'd disappear. She would urgently drop whatever she was doing to find me and with relief she would find me sitting in front of the television in awe as I watched a symphonic performance. I was completely in awe. As a baby, before I could hold my head up, when it was time for me to sleep I was not content with being held and rocked to sleep. You had to lay me down in the middle of the bed, turn on some soft music and let me be. My Mom not only fed me physically, she fed my soul with peace and music and it has remained so throughout my life. For a while I was the only child in the home so my imagination was sometimes my best friend. I spent a lot of time with myself getting to know me. Through books I journeyed to unknown places, I could escape there and as a result I was rather shy at times. I'd rather live vicariously through books. In school, I was able to shine in the classroom and most teachers saw something in me they believed in. It was in school that I learned more about the theatre and the art of drama and music together. It was fascinating and in my leisure time if I was not reading or writing, I was acting out scenes with my imaginary characters. My humble beginnings were based largely on things that were directly related to the arts and creativity. Both my Mom and my Aunt played piano. My Mom learned and moved on to the literary side of things, my Aunt moved on to playing piano and organ for a lifetime in church. My Mom's other sister played piano, violin and organ. Much of my family had the inclination to play or sing music.

Today I eat, breathe, and sleep music. My own personal Julliard came not by coincidence, but by design.

"Real life begins for me at a new place as I gracefully tread into my fifties."

CHAPTER TWO

WHEN DOVES FLY, SO DO I

It was 1999, the big Y2K scare had everyone unsure about whether this world of ours would survive the year 2000. People were thinking that the computers would crash and all would be devastation. Many people predicted the absolute worst. Yes, this was a strange situation that most of us had to face. The world was challenged to a new height as many people thought the world was coming to an end. Some thought that this would be the beginning of the end. I had my own personal thoughts about technology, doubtful that we were facing the absolute end. I could imagine, however, how wires might spring forth from every direction, like the cartoons depicted on the tele. The wires would go "boing" as the wires would carelessly fly hay-wire after equipment failure. Other than that, I had no worries about civilization coming to a complete halt. It was potential pandemonium that the world might spin on its axis in a terrible ball of confusion due to people's misconceptions. It was intriguing to hear the stories people concocted about what they thought would come to be. It was difficult to imagine the computer crashing to the point that everything would lock up, or lock down and civilization as we know it would be no more. Overall, I had no "real" concerns about the world leap into the year 2000. At the same token, I had a friend whom I loved dearly in Germany. It was suggested that we meet up, just in case we never got a chance to see each other again. This was a wonderful man I met on the beach in Bournemouth, England ten years past. I had mixed emotions about this particular meeting due to the current situation we faced. He stole my heart; he was beautiful inside and out. He invited me to Germany to celebrate the New Year with him, just in case. . .

I wasn't sure whether I should go or stay due to the given circumstances. As time passed, I knew I had to make a decision. I didn't trust myself to make an immediate decision because there were so many variables; so many possibilities. There were many factors that played into this. I had two young boys full of splendor and energy that I adored more than life itself. I could not bear to be separated from them for a long period of time. I also had hopes that this certain love of mine, would someday be an integral part of our family tree. So, on one hand for me to travel to Germany, so far from my babies, there was a hopeful thought that my friend and I could establish a way for us. To have an everlasting relationship meant everything to us at the time. We had high hopes of endurance with hopes to propel ourselves to a higher level on our journey. A potential journey to forever. Just as long as we were together for just a little while in the midst of all the crazy predictions, we could somehow experience a joyful time of loves paradise. We were so in love in hopes for a brighter forever. So, I prayed and I prayed, asking the Creator of the Universe to help me by showing me what I must do. Now mind you, I am one of those people who might very well look over those quiet little indications, those subtle hints that might give me a piece of this intricate puzzle, a clue. Those hints had to be rather abrupt sometimes, especially when I am not paying close attention. After days of calling for the Master to guide and direct me, I got sidetracked as I often do when seeking an answer from him.

The boys had just come home from school one day. I was preparing them for homework and a snack, when the doorbell rang. It was the neighbor who brought some homemade tortillas she'd promised. We talked briefly, had a laugh or two before saying our good-byes. As I turned to go back to tend to the children, I saw a glimmer of light which seemed to be coming from the ground. It seemed as if a reflection of light, hit a dew drop on a blade of grass at the perfect angle. It was astonishing as it called me to action. I wasn't sure if my eyes were playing tricks on me. This glimmer sparked my curiosity; it had the best of me. Knowing fully that I needed to get back to my motherly duties, I could not help myself. I paused to see where this light was coming from.

As curiosity continued to call my name, I walked out the front door and down the long pathway to the driveway. At the cornered edge, there was a little tip of something nestled in the dirt so deeply, I knew it had been there for quite some time. I reached towards this glimmering impression, submerged in the dirt. Investigating with my fingernail, I had to pry it from the solid ground. At this point, I find myself tugging away at this manifestation of light. Out came the most beautiful message as clear as could be! It was a little dirt covered, plastic replica of a tiny bird. As I examined this precious little bird, cleaning off the mud, I realized that it had an iridescent hue; it was a dove! Immediately I understood the message was certain. It was clear that everything was going to work out just fine. What a profound moment; a "go ahead" spoke clearly to me. The light of the dove opened up its message to me to let me know that I had the green light to go forth. It was the voice of God that gave me assurance. I had no doubt that I would have traveling mercies, the children would be fine, and that I would come back to the family safely. So, I faithfully went to commence upon a celebration of a lifetime. Excitedly I ventured into the New Year 2000 with a certain zest for life I had not experienced before. What a miraculous gift, just for me at that moment. With this assurance, I packed my bags, grabbed my passport, kissed my babies, prayed and kissed my babies some more. Off I flew to Germany with confidence and a sense of peace. With eagerness to fly, I was overjoyed and my spirits were soaring.

The trip was one that I shall never forget. He and I celebrated the coming in of the New Year on the Rhine River where there were thousands of people in their beautifully tailored winter coats and hats and mittens. Crowds of people everywhere had bottles of spirits while enjoying their loved ones as we embarked upon the New Year 2000 with all of its uncertainties. In Koln, people joyfully anticipated the New Year coming. It was as if this was just another ordinary New Year festivity, full of jubilance and cheer. Grand historical monuments strategically placed, brightly lit and mounted on huge platforms in the middle of the river for everyone to admire. There was so much to see and the sights were spectacular to behold. There was a stage set up with a rock band playing "Ole Lang Syne." It was the wildest, yet the best version I'd ever heard. Astonished by the moment in time, I could hardly take it all in. With all the theatrical creativity I could muster, I in a bright blue boa made of ostrich feathers made my grand entrance. I stuck out like a sore thumb in the crowd. I was so uniquely different I thought I should be the grandest diva of them all. I was, if only in my own mind. I considered myself a thespian so it was necessary for me to play the part in its entirety. We met on a United Kingdom tour, so he expected a bit of flamboyance. He seemed to celebrate our differences, coming from two different ends of the earth. It was amazing to know that my loved one basked in the fact that I could be happy, free and me while daring to be different. He was my love, my all in all who allowed me to just be. We were in love. We danced the night away and laughed ourselves into oblivion. Oh, what a time we had.

The next day, we were scheduled to attend a meeting in London. It was all vacation for me, but business and pleasure for him. Although I could barely speak any German at all, he spoke enough English to muddle through, we managed to have a splendid time together I understood him and he understood me, even in our silences. Sometimes I reminisce about our experiences, many of which surpassed words. To communicate like we did, beyond mere words was another level of intimacy completely.

We knew our hotel was on the Thames River but we had no idea what our view would be like. We were hopeful that we might have a glass reflection of lights to amuse us. When we arrived to our suite, we dropped our bags, embraced and together walked directly to the window in anticipation. When we opened the curtains, we could not believe our eyes! The enormous London Bridge looked close enough to touch. We stood there in utter shock for minutes, unaware of the time. This was part of my dream series. Some dreams come true and have the ability to change one's life.

Our journey had come full circle. The vacation ended in the very place we met some years before. It was a most perfect resolve. We were love birds who took a chance on our happiness. We never know what the future holds until we take a chance to find out.

I will always remember that When Dove's fly, So Do I.

"I will always remember that when doves fly, so do I."

CHAPTER THREE
REFLECTIONS OF LIGHT

I was invited to Germany as a special guest soloist by a dear friend. I was expected to meet with more than a 100-voice choir. I arrived during rehearsals and the excitement filled the air in all directions. Seemingly no one was very fluent in English with the exception of my friend and the Director. They sang mainly traditional spiritual songs, intended for performance in a near-by cathedral. Upon arrival, the feeling was warm and inviting. I found it so gratifying to come to a place where music was our means of communication. Music is truly a language of its own with an ability to bring all people together.

The rehearsal took place in a small rural area where I was told that some people had only seen black people on television. I wondered what that might feel like. It was a quaint little town without sidewalks. The roads were bumpy as we ventured through cobblestone streets. It was a special time of anticipation, because I knew exactly what my mission was. I envisioned myself building a gap between two cultures that were miles apart yet so much alike. One of the vehicles in which we could travel was this imaginary musical bridge I'd envisioned where harmonious encounters would take place. This bridge would transcend words and sounds so that our spirits could meet on a mutual plane. I witnessed the readiness in their eyes. As I sang, I could see the warmth and the love on the faces of the people. The meeting was golden and the mission accomplished.

Afterwards, my friend brought one particular woman to meet me personally. She was a bit older than me, maybe in her 50s, with a classy, cute haircut. As he interpreted her introduction, I noticed her face became flush as she was getting very emotional. As she continued to explain, I learned that she was a recent cancer survivor. She looked amazing to have undergone all the chemotherapy and such. Just looking into her eyes told a story of pain and victory all in one. I could see so much without interpretation. In silence, we were connected. She went on to tell me about a dream she had the night before. This miraculous woman had a premonition of an African woman that sang with a voice from the heavens. She said that she didn't understand how she should interpret the dream until she came face to face with me. Even though she hadn't had a very close relationship with God, she said that during her fight to survive she had come to get to know Him in a personal way. In order to draw closer to Him, she decided to join this choir. Her walk was getting stronger with Him daily. She knew that night that God was a God of healing, of miracles and of vision.

*****

This woman was an absolute angel. She delivered a powerful message of hope and love to me. Glory filled the room. She helped me to understand just how much we need one another and how much love there is to absorb rather than hate. This meeting profoundly moved me. It reminded me that nothing is by coincidence, it is meant to be. Even when some things look grim, there is a reason that cannot always be explained immediately. It is important that we trust our higher power to guide and direct our path. It is not always in our immediate circle that we find messages, but around the globe every day, every hour, everywhere. He is omnipotent and teaching us every step of the way. With so much hatred in the world, we have the ability to reach across invisible barriers and lines of disharmony. In order to reach a common ground of understanding, the differences of culture and/or religion are of no consequence. I still envision a garden of harmonious, blended colors. This will remain in my heart for always and I thank God for the lesson that day.

Enlightenment

As Perfumed air loomed in the dim lit room, I sat reminiscing over the day's events. I was driving on a normal day, doing everyday errands when a spark of life energy came upon me. I had to pull over and absorb all that was happening to my spirit. I was beyond words. I got this overwhelming sense of sweetness as if my heart was getting a massage. This unusual sensation was so strong that it brought me to tears. I remember being close to a high school when it happened. It was as close to what people describe as Euphoria as I can imagine it to be. Maybe this is part of the grieving process, I don't know. It is not for me to question. All I need to know is that it was a gift. This sensational embrace lasted only for a couple of minutes. This feeling came and went so quickly, I encountered a divine understanding that I had been touched by the spirit of God. It was a sense of well-being, of wholeness. It was an abundance of tender comfort that came over me like a warm blanket of water all over my body. My heart felt like it was immersed in peaceful flowing waters for a few fleeting moments, I was in a blissful state of ecstasy. Maybe it was pure ecstasy, but whatever it was, the feeling was at the top of its class. If it were a light, at least a tangible one, its brilliance would have outshined the sun. I pondered about what it could be and then let go of my quandary and just let it be. The feeling I experienced was far better than any of the questions I had.

Everything was still and as pure as it should be in that instant. That moment in time was so precious that anyone should be so fortunate to see or experience anything remotely close to that ever in life. For whatever reason, God chose me to shed His light upon. I am full of love and gratitude forever more as a result of this miraculous gift bestowed upon me. Maybe it was the precursor for something more. For that moment, it was perfect and it was precise. I had encountered enlightenment and it left me without words. I basked in the moment as it lingered for a brief time. Overcome with emotion, I started back to my daily routine at work. I knew something good was sure to come. I didn't know when or from whom, but I had been visited by a divine presence and I understood that good was expected to come.

----Some wonderful angels watching over me.

CHILDREN OF LIGHT

Shortly after this encounter, I met the sweetest little girl who I picked up as a client. She hopped in the front seat with me and I was blown away by her familiarity. It made me wonder whether she wasn't a long-lost relative. She was blond, she was smart and adorable, but most importantly she was walking in the "light." This young lady may have been 17 or so, but she was full of wisdom and brilliance. Her effervescence fascinated me as if she were an old kindred spirit. We immediately started a dialogue that was comforting. We talked about our God given ability to read peoples body language and facial expressions. In addition to reading people, we talked about another subject very dear to my heart: clairvoyance. It is something that one cannot always explain but we know that it reaches far beyond the five-sensory contact. We talked about the fact that we mutually acknowledged that in one another. We had many things in common, great exchanges we shared. Before we were finished on our journey together, she told me how interesting my stories were and how she thought I should write a book. I couldn't imagine what motivated her to say such a thing as I looked at her in astonishment. I asked her why she said that and she responded by telling me that it sounded as if it could be a book. I thought to myself, that this young woman has intuition that she is unaware of............" I was sort of thinking out loud and sharing some of my thoughts for the book. She was completely unaware of that fact in the natural. In the spirit realm, however, she was directly in tune. This bright light of a girl came to remind me that I was not to ponder nor procrastinate, rather to finish because I had much to say. There were several messages coming from all directions. They came from friends I knew and a few I didn't know. Such is the case here. Not by coincidence, rather by design. Its Un-real how these messages, some subtle and some not so, are coming into view. This baby girl could not have been more than a young pup; as cute as she could be. She shared most intimately with me about how huge her compassion was for those less fortunate, how it overtook her body to the point of tears. We talked about my work in transportation and how I felt so instrumental in the community. I told her I see this job as a ministry to help people. It gives me freedom to be me without stress and to touch the lives of people who need it most. Touching lives in a special way was the best healing for me while I was in my grieving stages after my Moms transition. She agreed that even though she knew how dangerous it was to pick up strangers while driving, she was moved by people along the highway of life who asked her for rides and/or needed one. When she was able she picked up many strangers and helped them get to their destination. She said that she knew instinctively the good people. I admired her courageous attitude. She talked extensively about how she could see someone less fortunate and feel their anguish. She was often moved to pray for long periods of time for those in need. I shall never forget my little Angel spirit friend; she came to share an invaluable lesson of compassion and neither of us were aware that this encounter was to take place in such a profound way.

Every day, I get these precious little messages. My third eye, my pineal gland is opening at such an alarming rate it is most amazing. I believe it to be called enlightenment or an awakening. I believe that my life is coming into focus now more than ever. To be able to live on a platform that will allow me to impart wisdom and love to people all over is a privilege. I realize now that it is not in our time that these impartations of enlightenment should come. When God gives it to us, it cannot be taken away and it is only for that certain individual. I believe I've arrived in some degree to a place that will blossom even more, so that I can pass it on to someone who may be in need. The beauty is in the lesson; it is a gift for the taking. When we get silent we can begin to tap into it.

Everyone we meet has a purpose in our life if only for a fleeting moment in time. We don't always realize the purpose of someone coming into our lives especially if it is not a "bright light" experience, but it is valuable just the same. A little soul searching requires that we quiet the voices in our heads and get to the quiet, tranquil place where the Master can commune and sup with us. It is ours for the taking.

If this young woman never crosses my path again, I will forever remember how this precious one came to bring a quickening in my spirit. She was----A REFLECTION OF LIGHT.

"A Reflection of Light"

"Look up and keep your head lifted to the sky."

CHAPTER FOUR
20th Street Blues

PRELUDE

This has been the most difficult subject to talk about and confront. It has been a hidden feeling I've lived with for a very long time.

The arduous task of weight loss has been an incredible journey. This has been a struggle all my life and finally the struggle is no more. It has been a "Goliath" in my life for many years and just like life itself, there is always going to be a huge challenge to face along the way. This was mine. This so-called Goliath was characterized in my mind as a giant mountain to climb with slippery, rocky places which resulted in many cuts, bruises, insect bites, sun burn, dangerous turns and snakes to detour my path. It was a process of numerous baby steps until this day.

*****

I've been a large sized girl all of my life. I was always in the top five or ten percent of my class academically, but in another area, I felt I didn't fit in at all. (At some points on this journey, I felt like a total failure) Instead, I stood out like a sore thumb and considered myself a big-boned, oversized, high yellow girl. Some classmates would refer to me as "high Yellow" and some would say I was just a girl with big bones. I didn't resist, that way it didn't seem so bad. I wasn't always fond of being categorized that way, but that softened the blow and I accepted it. I had some very awkward years as a youth. I was shy and I would have been satisfied with my head in a book somewhere when out in public or in school, but it wasn't always a practice of social etiquette to do so. I thought being somewhat shy and removed, that no one would pay attention to me (publicly), that is. Once again, I was mistaken. Instead, it was quite the opposite. There always felt like a light incessantly beaming down on me and as much as I did not want it and tried to dim it, the brighter it became.

Raised with a religious background as an Adventist, we were taught that we must take care of our "temples." In doing so, I grew up with a significant teaching about keeping our bodies clean. Did I always follow it? No, but it was a guideline that I always measured by. Learning from International cook books, I went on a journey to create my own path. Since time can remember, even playing in the mud (cooking in my "pretend kitchen"), I was always curious about different combinations of things which resulted in a lot of experimentation. In the process, I'd make up all kinds of concoctions from the earth in my so-called cooking element. Potions then, I call it alchemy now. I've always been a person to branch off the path that everybody else followed. Following my own health practice infused with Adventism; I learned and incorporated all types of herbs, supplements, yoga, Tai Chi, different philosophies and the like. I read a book referred by a dear friend who lived upstairs from me on 20th Street called, "Back To Eden" by Jethro Kloss, (highly recommended), that helped me on this journey. I experimented with fasts, diets, bathing techniques, ointments and natural remedies and potions all of which were fascinating to me. As adventuresome as I am and as much as I enjoy exploring the way things work, I took on a lifelong venture. During my trial and adventure, I was enjoying the process of learning and growing. I didn't worry too much about a little weight gain in the process. My ideas ran rampant. It allowed me to step over the portal into a whole new way of looking at life. Gee, I thought I was dealing with a weight problem then. Even though, my family always leaned towards healthier food choices and lifestyle, there was something about seeking my own path that opened the window to my own personal preferences. I was proud to be the first one in my family to venture into the world of vegetarianism as I have always been a self-starter, kind of girl.

*****

Looking back in retrospect, I think because I tried so many things, my body didn't know how to process much of it. I was becoming increasingly heavier although my goal was to become healthier. As I learned a lot I began to slowly gain weight instead of lose. If I hadn't been dancing with the televised Soul Train crew every week consistently, I probably would have been in worse shape. Gradually, I regretfully owned my big girl status and carried on. Somehow, I carried a bit of confidence with me along the way. This confidence would have its peaks and valleys but it was not a big worry because it didn't stop the fellas from coming around so I thought I was doing fairly well.

*****

My father once bought a Sweat shirt for me that said, "If I can't win, I don't want to play." I really thought I was winning for the most part. Well, I was winning! At least I thought so. That was my motto in a nut shell. I tried this for a while and then began to delve into the magazines like many teens and found that all the models were anorexic skinny. I knew I didn't want that, but in comparison, I was starting a bulge that I grew a little more concerned about as time traveled. I aspired to be like them (with a little extra), so I started on this journey of dieting. Many young women find this path very difficult; I was one of the millions of young women dealing with the same issues. Looking back in retrospect, I probably messed up my system during that time with experimenting and tampering with normal bodily functions as a teen; I confused my body and lost my way as I digressed. In other words, I screwed up! I didn't gain another two scores until after my first child birth. It was worth it completely, because of the wondrous gift I received. Finding my way back has been a long arduous journey. Someone once said that comparison is the thief of all happiness.

*****

Consequently, I dug a deep hole which has cost me time, aggravation and frustration. Did I say a few tears? This battle became an internal struggle which went on for years and years in silence. What a lonely road to travel, when the road is arduous and most difficult. No one knows the inside. When I found myself at my highest weight of 289 pounds, I became desperate. I fought long and hard, while raising a family. It seemed to be a Goliath that I could not conquer. I prayed, I cried internally as I didn't like my physical body. I felt as if I failed myself. It was most difficult preparing meals for my family and not being able to partake. So, I did partake of mine and sometimes theirs too! It was a snowball effect that wasn't stopping. I began to worry about my health but there was a nervous anxiety that kept me eating my life away.

*****

One day at my lowest ebb, I didn't know where to turn. I thought this it! I've got to do something desperate. I never had a feeling of hopelessness like I did on this particular day. I hit my bottom. Never before would I succumb to the mere thought of operations like current day trends. I thought it was considered taking the lazy way out and that I had given up on myself, if I had to resort to something like that. I was determined to conquer Goliath in my own way, in my own time which never worked. I had finally surrendered to the idea that I would have to go get surgery. I was feeling alone in a lonely, dark den of hopelessness. I went downstairs to tell my son what I was thinking. He said one word that changed my thinking immediately and I felt ashamed of even thinking those kinds of thoughts. I said to him, "Son I'm thinking of going to seek counseling for the weight loss surgery." He replied, "Ah Mom that's cheating!" I knew he was right. I taught my sons that cheating was worse than lying. So, when he fed it back to me, I received it wholeheartedly and that is all I needed to squash that idea immediately. The only problem that remained was that I had no solution, at least not yet. I still felt like I was hiding so much of me under the guise of a larger than life me. It was simply uncomfortable in my skin being so heavy. No one knows the mental anguish that one endures. It was a dangerous place to be. Any person telling you that they are in the best of health and happy being over more than 50 pounds over- weight is fooling themselves. I believe that the body is not at its healthiest. I also believe that the mental health isn't as it should be if we are in a place of denial. Your movement is impeded, your breath is compromised and your esteem is lower than it could be. As long as I had someone to take care of, I had an excuse not to take care of myself.

*****

After my Mom passed, I found that I had no one to take care of anymore. My children were grown, my love was gone and it never occurred to me that it was time to take care of myself. Once I got a chance to be alone with myself, I began to start an arduous search for things that I liked. Getting quiet and still was the best thing I could have done for myself. It was a time of true reflection of who I am and what I needed to do for me. At this point, I was forced to work on my own life's trajectory with a huge part of it being more health consciousness. Finding my way back to myself was quite a journey. Through trials, sorrow, tears and a tremendous amount of pruning, it has been a heartwarming experience, however challenging. God said, "I see you and I haven't forgotten about you." In this, I'd forgotten about Him. The good book tells us to take care of our temples. I overlooked that part completely and made a mess in my world. When I find a solution, even in a painful situation, I can also find joy. I still have a long way to go to get to my ideal weight but I found a place of well-being in my soul through the love of Christ, my church family and constant prayer. You see, it is all in how you think about things. Finding my way back to my essence has not been filled with cherry colored roses, rather I have a sense of peace that one cannot pay for. I joined a book club that teaches one how to properly nourish the body with a blend of fruits and vegetables with flax seed and protein to combat cravings and carbohydrates in a way that I thought was impossible. It is basically a raw whole food lifestyle.

I started buying all whole foods and I began to adopt a picture of health that was nothing less than amazing. It started with 10 days and continued as a lifestyle. It's been 2 months now, and my eating lifestyle has changed dramatically. My palate is different and things that are not good for me taste that way, NO GOOD! As a result, I don't eat the things that used to be so good to the taste and dangerously fattening. On my journey continuing on, I am moving in a direction that has changed my life completely. I am grateful to God for seeing me through such a challenge. The one thing I was sure to be consistent about was to keep the hope in me alive even when things seemed so cloudy and gray. Perseverance is what is important. It is not always easy to find viable solutions to a problem especially when you get to the very bottom of the challenge. Hold on to what you believe and never give up although it may look like a dead-end journey to hell. Never give up on your dreams. Our good health is a gift and often it is taken for granted. Whether the health issue is eating or physical ailments, just know that 89% of it is attitude and the way in which we face our challenges. Always helping someone else and neglecting yourself is never the answer. Self-preservation is the first law of nature.

In Conclusion: I threw away my scales, I gave up wanting it so bad and just decided to be healthy. Let Go and Let God!

<u>ONE DAY IN TIME</u>

My mothers' two sisters were very influential in my early years. I was taught to be a "good girl," which meant I was to be modest in my mannerisms and in my appearance. My perception of modesty through the eyes of my elders was taken to an extreme as a youngster. In searching for myself, there were times I wanted to crawl inside of myself without coming out unless I was completely compelled to do so. In addition to being bashful, I was self-conscious about my over-sized body which usually brought unnecessary attention. I had breasts blossoming and other parts of my anatomy, blossoming at an alarming rate. Suddenly, I was living in a woman's body as a teenager and there were times when I was awkwardly confronted by curious boys. My Aunts were women who always wore their dresses below the knee because it was the "modest" way to dress. I could imagine puritans or the Amish people walking amongst us.

The truth is I grew bashful about showing my legs. I would wear things around the house that might show my legs on occasion, but never outside in public. I rarely showed my legs even indoors. I would not be caught past the front door. I often felt as if I were completely naked; I wouldn't dare!!!!

Anything above the knee was out of the question for me. For me, Seventh-Day Adventism was synonymous with plain, boring and obscure and Amish like. That was the way I was expected to conduct myself as a "good Christian girl." So, I always had this picture in my head about what a girl like me was expected to act like, dress like, etc. I expected that of others that called themselves Christians until I grew because that was all I knew growing up. (Another chapter)

As of late, I was asked by my girlfriend to help with her Valentines' Dinner Dance project. I was happy to help. A few months before the show I found a bat-wing dress that was a little tight and the hem line was slightly above the knee. Needless to say, I immediately thought it was a bit too much for me to consider. I pondered for a while because I truly liked the dress. To even consider a dress like this was completely out of character for me. My ration was that I would lose a little weight and the dress would somehow be a bit longer and I could wear the dress. Too many times have I quietly whispered this to myself. Well, when the day came, I almost chickened out! I hadn't lost the intended weight and I was truly nervous about being half naked, so I felt.

It occurred to me that maybe I should have become a Nun and then I quickly came to my senses and thought that just because I was indoctrinated to think this way, didn't mean that I was any less modest, nor did it mean that I was doing anything wrong.

Courageously, I told myself that I am not a Puritan. No. That was hardly the case;

"No one would know how I was feeling deep inside."

—I was a well-rounded, voluptuous woman that had a lot to give, who was terrified to show her legs! Insanity, I thought. Once I faced that fact, I talked myself into the idea that I should wear this dress and no one would know exactly how I was feeling deep inside, except me. Actually, one of my besties knew, but that is it. I knew I would be uncomfortable.

It wouldn't have been so bad, if I could mingle in with the crowd and not be noticed, but it was a night I had to be on stage so there was no getting around the fact that I would be seen by all. I had to pretend that I was okay with it. I've been known to utilize my natural, God given acting skills to pull it off. I did not want to be embarrassed or indicate any sign of insecurity. I put a flowing, sheer jacket over the dress to make myself feel a bit more comfortable and off I went to the stage. I was more like a security blanket. The feeling of liberty was all over my countenance; it was thrilling. So, on Valentine's Day I was feeling something I'd never experienced which was exhilarating as if I'd been reborn. Maybe I had been in a way of speaking. Well, by taking this brave step, I discovered that I'd been missing out on yet another part of me that was dying to get out! Who knew? "Not I," said the shy little girl inside. My coming out party for myself was when I revealed my legs above the Knee; a public first. Gee whiz, one would think I was without clothes at all, which is sort of the way I felt when getting dressed for the event. With all the courage I could muster, I went out on that stage in total masquerade and realized something extraordinary. I loved it!

Weight always provided a way of hiding for me and I wasn't fully aware of it completely until that day, as a full-grown adult! I was always wondering what it might be like to step out of my shell completely. Now even though most people tend to think I am bold and boisterous, fun, happy and full of sunshine there is an absolute little girl in me. This little girl has been sheltered all her life inside this full-figured body as I like to think of it. Perception is not always reality. There was always this inside little voice that said you cannot be the best you, unless there is a significant amount of weight loss involved. On the inside however, I've been encapsulated by my thinking and not honestly dealing with these feelings head on. From that very moment forward, I'd been liberated just like that! Little life lessons keep coming and I cannot record them all fast enough. After this night of coming out to the world, I shifted into a knowingness that the thoughts we sometimes formulate due to outside influences, isn't always necessarily so. Yes, it is essential that we take care of our bodies and get fit, but we mustn't be crippled by the perception that magazines, media and television portray. Perception once again is not always what it is cracked up to be and neither is what you are taught. Our parents do the best they can, but through pathology sometimes the mark from your parents is not necessarily the mark for you. We must find our very own paths as we move through this thing called life. I took my shy self and placed "her" on the shelf. Meanwhile, a Zumba partner suggested that I join a support group of like-minded people who follow a famous nutritionist on how to rid the body of toxins and while obtaining optimum health at the same time. Still wanting to do it my way, I was warmly embraced by a group of like-minded people, who had a common goal. Ultimate fitness, optimum health and life longevity were a few mutual goals we were all aspiring to. I was searching for them and didn't even know it. To find that kind of support was like finding an umbrella in an unforeseen rain-forest. Although this is a Facebook following and I cannot see them face to face, it's the understanding about the way we look at food that keeps me motivated and somewhat accountable.

*****

About two weeks later, I started the program. My life of transformation had already begun to unfold. It was Monday and I knew it was time. I was taking baby steps that led up to this moment because I'd already been eating very little meat products. I had stopped eating most processed foods other than cheese, with which I was trying desperately to eliminate. I was careful with sodium and sugars yet wanting to exclusively eat raw vegetables and fruit. "Any old Monday will do as a starting day" I said, even though I cannot begin to tell how many Monday's I started and stopped. As I began, I felt 100% energized as my body rid itself of foods with very little nutrients in my body. I slept like a baby kitten and I started noticing immediate results. I lost 10 pounds in the first week. I finally found the answer. This search has been going on for a very long time; the time has come. It was a vulnerable place of emotional roller-coasting as I began this journey moving through this process of releasing weight and inches, it still is. Today, I have the courage to move through it step by step. There is a shame that I feel when I think about how I hid myself for all these years. Nothing seemed to work until now. I tried so many diets, fads, under doctor's supervision, considerations, heartaches, weight clinics, etc. I feel marvelous darling. Remember, I said that the solution is in the way you think about things. When we change our thinking, our bodies will react accordingly. Someone once said that you cannot keep doing the same things while expecting different results. All these baby steps compiled themselves into one large adult step! Eating correctly will change the way you think. It will change your energy level as well as regulate your sleeping habits. Even my vision has improved. I now envision bigger things. I was able to grab a mental sling shot to conquer Goliath once and for all.

"It is never a coincidence."

Chapter Five
Dear Mr. Fleming: the day we met

After coming from Southern California to Northern, I started a new occupation. My younger brother came to visit me one day and he was using a new aged taxi cab service as his transportation. I thought it rather daring and very odd that he would use anything other than a traditional taxi for transportation. After all, riding around with strangers is dangerous, isn't it? After a year or two, he started working for this company. I watched his progress as it afforded him a new car. "I was proud of his immediate success." After I talked to him more about it, he suggested I give it a go. With a certain amount of uncertainty, I assessed my prior experience. I could not pick-up strangers as if I were a taxi cab driver. I asked myself the question, *"Who me? Mz. Marcy as a driver, I don't think so."* There isn't the slightest chance that I would consider letting anyone get in my car that I didn't know. Being a girlie kind of girl, I thought this was work for guys only. Be careful what you say you won't do. This was a time of transition in my life after losing my dearest loved one. It was time to re-invent myself. So, I started to consider options.

Daring myself to take the challenge, I tried it as terrified as I was. Fast forward, it has been such a journey to the extent that I must write another book on the series of events that have taken place. Shortly into my new line of work/adventure, I toured all over the California area. This particular day in Beverly Hills, I picked up a gentleman and his care provider at a hospital and took him home. It was a little frustrating in the hustle and bustle of the big city where I was born. Things had changed in the past 10 years; the traffic had increased and the area I was in was more congested than I remembered it to be, by far. Somehow, I kept circling the block over and again and I could not find these two passengers. After about 20 minutes of attempts with no success, I surrendered and decided that I would cancel the ride due to such difficulty. Something in me would not let me cancel. It was the oddest thing. Once I finally got them in the car, I acknowledged why I needed to help this duo. He was a lovely, well to do gentleman who assumed a position of eminence. He exuded grandeur and poise. It appeared that he had recently experienced some health challenges. I was so pleased to be in a position to help this distinguished soul who gently demanded respect. I could tell he had been very successful as he was conducting business while I transported him to his home. The kind gentleman lived in an exclusive area called "Over-hill," which is an exclusive all black neighborhood that has a panoramic view overlooking the city. I had not been to this part of the city for years and had almost forgotten about it. It had been so long since I had the feeling of warmth and hospitality in our neighborhood. The houses were groomed to perfection and great pride filled the air. There was a certain charm about this neighborhood and I thought I would meander around a bit. It was about time for my auto to be serviced. I felt this was the ideal time to check in with "my folks." I ventured into the heartbeat of the community where there was a certain rhythm on the street. The Horns were honking, people talking, laughing and hustling about. Big bottomed Sisters with their pants painted on, brothers winking and trying to get a phone number while the Old folks waved at familiar faces. It was like the Hyde Park or Covent Gardens of South Central which made the day perfect and complete. It was a wondrous sight to behold. When I stepped into the shop, I was amazed at all I saw. It was a movie scene that came to life. I immediately got my pen and pad and started to journal on the spot. The people in the lobby were talking as if they were having a networking party at someone's house. Everyone was laughing and exchanging good vibrations and their favorite car repair stories. Visualize a place where on the corner you find a Mom and Pop shop serving Fried Chicken with hot fries and hot sauce. Then next door there was a row of establishments: a barber shop, a plant store, a tee-shirt shop that sold CDs, a store front that had exotic body oils and incense billowing onto the street. Finally, the traditional beauty supply place owned by Asian folk who dared to be in the community with a nail shop in the back.

While waiting for my car, there was a soul food restaurant across the driveway. I could smell the wondrous aromas drifting my way. As I continued to absorb all this exuberance, my spirits grew higher than before. My hands could not produce fast enough nor interpret the liveliness that overwhelmed my countenance. A pleasant younger man came in and handed me a card. The card he offered was for a grand opening being held across the way. I was delighted to find that this card was an invitation to the restaurant. Without hesitation, I went in and was greeted with warm, southern hospitality. A family run, operation and even though these people were complete strangers, it felt like coming home to long lost relatives. I had not been around this environment in quite a long time. I felt a warm embrace the moment I set foot in the place. As I walked in, I noticed an elderly gentleman relaxing and I assumed he was the grandfather of the business. He was casually dressed with hat on, tilted just so. It looked as if he had been dozing as he was very relaxed. When he looked over and spoke to me, with a quiet, gentle, distinctive accent, I imagined this well-mannered, familiar stranger was from the South. He had a wonderful peace about him, and as the staff brought me a cold glass of lemonade we began the beguine. This grandfather had an aura of calm that could not be overlooked. I immediately felt a warm embrace. In fact, his very presence lured me in. As we began to converse, I knew immediately that this was by design, that this would not be our only encounter. A rare jewel in our community sat before me. I don't think anyone else had noticed besides me as it felt as if I was sitting amongst royalty, yet for everyone else he was just dad. How could that be? It took me by surprise as I whipped out my notepad with his permission. Little did I know that we both would soon have tears streaming down our faces as our souls met? It was a divine appointment.

A JEWEL IN OUR PRESENCE

We engaged as reflections of the past arose and I was drawn to him. He had my full attention as he began to reminisce on days gone by. I had to stop and pick up my bottom lip from the floor when he said, "….as I was policing the policemen." I couldn't write fast enough. By the time my car was ready maybe twenty minutes or so into the conversation, we were fully engrossed in the momentary interview. I thanked the attendant and continued our conversation, "she should be on her way." There was no small chance that I was close to being done with this amazing soul. His words loudly reverberated in my head. That portion of his statement jumped out at me in an exaggerated fashion. Tears of anguish rolled down our cheeks as we thought about the condition our world is facing. We cried about the fact that no one seemed to have the courage and the fortitude anymore after the late great Dr. King set the precedence for all people; in many ways, we digressed as a people. Oh yes, we had a meeting of the souls that day. After we wiped our tears and began to laugh through them, he said, "For a man to cry was not a sign of weakness because Jesus wept in the garden of Gethsemane and at the grave of Lazarus. He wept at the condition of Jerusalem. So, if Jesus wept, who are we to condemn others?"

Mr. Fleming and I continued a most intimate talk about racism and injustice all over the world and focused particularly here in the great old US of A. We laughed at the irony of those who make the rules and regulations and how ridiculous they can be while enforcing "the Law." I didn't want to interrupt him, but I had to know as I asked him to kindly elaborate on his previous statement. He so willingly took me on a journey I shall never forget. He began to relive his fight for justice on Venice Beach. He said that there were many black folks that migrated from Arkansas and other parts of the South in the early 1900s. In 1956, he moved to Broadway Blvd., in Venice Ca. I was unaware that this was a place of escape for many families, especially those coming from the South. He told me about a little apartment he had at the very edge of the alley where many injustices took place. These injustices were with law enforcement (predators) vs. Neighborhood Residents of the area. He reminisced about that entire scene, frame by frame. The policemen would surround a person or persons and brutally assault common law-abiding citizens in hopes that no one would witness the account. As they moved in on their prey like vultures, Mr. Fleming would rush gallantly into the alleys with a camera rolling. The camera was his weapon of defense against the police and their barbaric, bloodthirsty ways in the streets. I imagined a show like Hawaii-Five-O, or Miami Vice with Mr. Fleming head lining as the star of the show.

This was his fascinating, real life story. So many days and nights he found himself witnessing police men savagery against innocent brothers and sisters of the community. He vehemently fought to help and protect his people. Although he indefatigably stood for justice, he too had an encounter with several police officers because he would not cower at their intimidation tactics. At the age of 57, a male and a female officer accosted him and beat him down to the ground, within inches of his precious life. He was prepared to die for justice at all costs for the love of his people. The heinous beating did not stop his vigilance one bit. Shortly after this incident, with fresh courage and renewed zeal, he wrote this poem for the world to see.

The Verdict

"My name is Shearwood Fleming, the story I'm about to tell you is true. It happened to me, it could happen to you. On May 6, of 94, five white racist cops decided they would put on a show. I wasn't doing anything as they could plainly see. Not only did they beat me but they pepper-sprayed me. Two years later we took the case to court, all the jury was of no support. My lawyer stepped up to the podium, stating the facts of my case, then the judged yelled out, 'this is not about race!' Even the picking of the jury one black out of eight, the defense attorney made sure he didn't stay. Even the ruling of the verdict for those lying cops. Can't you see the madness hasn't really stopped? Yes, hearing the reading of the verdict was hard to absorb, but let me tell you that my lawyer really did his job. Was I disappointed or was I leery? I know'd I couldn't trust an all-white jury. And after the reading of the in just verdict was in, some of the jurors came over to try to shake my hand. But after 500 years of racial injustice how could a handshake heal and correct it? But when something negative in the news about Hispanics and blacks they show pictures and descriptions what we look like, but when it comes to whites, no matter how gruesome it is or how bad it sounds, the media will always find some kind of way to tone it down."

*****

Mr. Fleming was born in Hill House, Mississippi as a sharecroppers' son. He was an errand boy with 4 brothers and 2 sisters. He lived modestly in a loving household of nine. His father was a carpenter, a fisherman and an excellent business man. A dutiful wise husband and father was he. To provide for his family, he raised cattle, hogs and chickens. His Mother was a housewife and very delicate woman. As a young man Sherwood helped his father tend to the animals and tended the farm: milking the cows, cutting wood for fire shucking corn for the hogs and chickens, slop for the hogs. He helped his family harvest food; such as potatoes and peanuts. They called it, "The Truck Patch," country sayings.

His father taught him many wise colloquialisms, prose and short stories. These things began to weave the fabric of his young life and stuck with him along life's highway.

"On the wellest day of your life, you are sick enough to die." --- unknown quote from his father.

"It's a long road that never ends and a bad wind that never changes and a front only lasts so long then it wears off."

"Push me when I'm falling, you kick me when I'm down, I guess I missed my calling because I should have been a clown." ------James Carr

"When He stands within me, I cannot stand by myself." Shearwood Fleming

He also recited the Serenity Prayer as mother would often share, which resonated in a very special way.

Shearwood was a good listener who began to gather and savor all the wisdom he could from his elders, teachers and those in authority. Although, he respected figures of authority, he realized early on, that some things were unjust and unfair. This became a great concern for him. As a young man, he was inspired by older students in school who memorized written pieces by famous activists and freedom fighters. The prowess with which his alumni spoke inspired him to do the same. Many academic subjects were not of interest nor was he extremely proficient in, however, his love was for the English language and literature overruled. Mr. Fleming was an excellent speller and had the gift of memorization. He championed most of the Spelling Bee competitions in school.

His parents gave him all the tools he needed to survive in a world that was not so kind to Negroes at the time. As a young man, he learned a great skill in recitation in school which is where it all began.

*****

As the words gently flowed from the depths of his soul, the incantations started and if I closed my eyes I could see and hear both Mr. Fleming and the late great Dr. Martin Luther King come forth simultaneously. I believed at that very moment that Dr. King was speaking through Mr. Fleming. It was amazing to see his entire stature change before my eyes. In his adult life, he has paid many tributes to the late Dr. King and received many great acknowledgements for his work on the streets of Venice. Here was this brilliant jewel in the neighborhood sitting before me who was an unsung hero of our time. I thought what a shame it would be to not share about a man who loved his people so extensively. He felt strongly about speaking up and encouraging others to speak out against those who imposed racial injustices to others.

Mr. Fleming had a love for young people that exceeded the norm. Although he was not a typical classroom teacher, he was a teacher just the same. Outraged at the condition we still face, he showed great concern for what the children of today will face. We agreed that in some ways we have advanced and in other ways the systemic injustices have been implemented in a way that sends us spiraling backwards.

ALRIGHT!

"There are those of you that started out with us got weary along the way lost your courage and quit. There are some of us that are still here today, we know it's not over yet. The journey is hard the journey is long our bodies are so tired but we must go on. Not for a movie, or a walk on part but at the end of life's journey there is a reward. Be honest with yourself, give reverence to God He will give you the victory whoever you are. In this world, there is not enough love and too much hate. The question is, "why do we run when God says wait!!!""

Cry a Few More Tears and you'll Be Home

Homeless in the street sleeping on bus benches sitting on hard seats.

Heavy hearted, swollen ankles and tired feet. I wasn't out there slippin' and trippin',

Rollin' blunts, smoking joints.

Now God has brought me to a place called turning point.

I was hurt by things that people would say but I went on from day to day. Knowing that God is always real He is that wheel in the middle of the wheel. Seem like I can hear the Master saying be strong my child, "Shearwood you're not alone, cry a few more tears and you'll be home."

The Beard Story

"The beard story you're about to hear is true. What I'm about to say is gonna sound kind of weird but there is a true story behind this beard. This beard is not a joke, I couldn't shave because my razor broke. Those ol' razors is hard to find, the only way to get them is to go online, and that takes time. So, the beard story is true and if you want to get the razor that's what you got to do."

*****

Mr. Fleming is a man of valor and sensitivity. His allegiance to his people is unmatched and he carries a special fondness for young people. With ambitious aspiration, he reaches out to our youth to share with them the soul connection between all peoples. His charm and great sense of humor leaves an esthetic quality that is undisputable. After being in his presence, I realize that I've been nourished by wisdom and grace.

In addition to memorization skills and invocation of great philosophers, this man reaches into the depths of his spirit and sings from his soul. He has the voice of life that can sing as well as recite and memorize like nothing one has seen before or since. God has carefully chosen this culmination of characteristics and placed them on Mr. Fleming and then sent me along to witness such magnificence. It is my privilege and utmost honor to be acquainted, however brief, with Mr. Shearwood Fleming.

"I am not going to step on nobody trying to get where I am trying to go. Let's join hands and go together." ----Mr. Shearwood Fleming

"Motherless Child"

"living within and without"

Chapter Six

MOTHERLESS CHILD

Once I met a lady from Japan in my Tai Chi class, who said that every day, every moment is a first for this time has never come before. She impressed upon me the importance of being in the present moment now. This is something that has always resonated deep within my soul. I find myself referring to phrases like, "Never have I experienced, or for the very first time I felt this way when it never occurred to me before now, or it seemed like the first time." Trying not to sound redundant, it is true that life is a revolving door. Experiences are unique and they seem to be new every time. These experiences are re-creations that are different every single time. The Tai Chi experience was even different after a year or more without it. This time I went through a series of bodily changes that were related to muscles that are not used very much. My body experienced pain and strength simultaneously. All I could do at that point was try to work right through it, the way I did when I lost my Mommy.

A dear fellow friend of mine came to visit me from out of town. He had never visited before or since, although looking back, nothing comes by coincidence. Since he was coming, I decided that I would visit Mom earlier in the day as we were making preparations for her to come home. Later that day, I planned a little outing for my friend as worried as I was about my Mom while quietly praying that she soon would be on the mend. The day was filled with mixed emotion when I could not get my Mom to eat her food anymore. Her last words to me were, "I hate to go to sleep on you like this." She went to sleep later on that evening. Even though I knew the end was drawing near, I was trying my best to prepare for the inevitable. Having lost my father a decade earlier, I knew what a difficult time was ahead. All I could imagine was how painstaking the experience had been when my father died and how much more strenuous losing my mom would be. I believed I would not be able to take a breath. I also believed that time would stop in its track and that I would not be able to take one step. The tender mercies of God came upon me on the day it happened.

My friend came into town sort of all of a sudden. I am not sure why it was designed for him to come because we never went out without being accompanied by mutual friends somehow. It just so happened, that he was the comfort that I needed at that time. My sister and I decided to go visit her son, my nephew, who was living in a super duper high rise full of glam and glitter. What a sight it was. It had a spectacular view; its aesthetic value was breathtaking. Usually on Friday nights, they had entertainment on the roof top, which provided a place to wind down after a week of hard work. That night I will never forget as there was no live music that particular night. Music of a different kind was about to play. I was greatly concerned and can't say I was having a good time, but I did my best to show my friend a nice time. As we mingled a bit, the song "Roof Garden" by Al Jarreau kept playing in my mind which was one of Mom and I's favorite Jarreau tunes. It was such a lovely view on a gorgeous star filled sky. Mom had a special place in her heart for Jarreau and so did I. She introduced so many fabulous musicians from her era to me. His musical legacy we mutually shared. After dinner time, I received a message to call the hospital. I thought nothing of it because I kept a close rapport with all the nurses on staff. Assuming it was routine check in about one thing or another, I returned the call. I searched to find a place of tranquility in the midst of all the action to respond. The voice on the other end changed my reality forever. It was the last and final call I would ever receive from the hospital on Mom's behalf. I sat there numb for just a moment, not knowing what to do. I slowly left the quiet room and went to my family and shared the news. My friend held me as I cried. He was compassionate and gave me so much comfort by reminding me that she would no longer endure suffering. I did not want to hear that but, I sure am grateful for his presence and his kind words. God knew exactly who should be there for me far better than I could ever imagine. Of all days, to be with my family through this crisis at this time, He set it up so perfectly, I know that there is NO COINCIDENCE. It is only by His grace and by His design that we have our being.

I knew I had to get to work and organize my thoughts as our family prepared for our last good bye. I was instantly placed in business mode. I was about my mother's business. Although, I was in the midst of devastation, I felt like my Mom had passed a torch of fire, strength, wisdom and forward fortitude directly to me so that I could undergo this task of publicly saying good-bye. I went to my brother and sisters house that night as I could not bear to be alone in that house. After all, we had been preparing the house for her return. When I got to the house to gather some things, I started a poem for Mom. The comfort of her spirit came to me immediately and even though, my perception of losing Mom made me believe I would not be able to speak, sing, walk, talk or breathe, it was not that way at all. Oddly, I became stronger instantly. As you will hear me say throughout this body of work, "perception is not reality," here lies a perfect example. Moms' greatest desire was for all of her children to come together in her name. We did the very thing Mom wanted; I believe we honored her in that way and we have continued to do so from this day forward. I am so grateful that we came together and remained together without confusion and strife as many families can be challenged by. I know my Mom would have stood taller than ever if she could see us now.

"Like dust sparkling, floating in the rays of sunshine, she awaits."
-----*Marcia Lewis*

God's Design

It's simply amazing how God places a design

How he orchestrates in His own perfect time

I could never begin to imagine what He has in store

And the magnitude of love He displayed as He opened the door

I was walking around trying not to wear a frown when a dear friend referred me to a job opportunity

As God would see fit, even in my doubt I could see a greater profundity

(As only He can do)

I accepted the challenge and with God's help, I found there an unexpected liberty. The favor He displayed for me was unbelievable and He promoted me in two months' time, almost inconceivable

But the power of the Master of the Universe displayed

An Awesome power that only He can convey. So, I wrapped up my two-bit knowledge, added with it a new awareness of medicines never heard of

Just in time to be with my Mom in her last days orchestrated by only the Master above

The job only lasted for a very short time before my mother's health took a drastic turn

Designed so perfectly I couldn't have been in a better position to serve

He placed His love in the palm of my hand so that I could administer to her the works of His Master Plan. -------*Marcia Lewis*

CATHARTIC

Sunday was my breaking point. I crossed a portal named Release. I finally accepted on Mother's Day at church of all places, that I needed to let go of holding on to my Mom who is no longer here. I couldn't accept the fact that she was actually gone until Mother's Day. I had a break down that took me to a place of uncontrollable tears, uncontrollable audible, noisy tears. It was a spiritual tugging on my inner man to let go, yet I resisted. Upon resisting I found my spirit getting weaker. The tears ran like a waterfall in an overflowing river below. As my strength appeared to falter someone ran to get a chair, the next person went to get water, one was praying, another fanning. A few people were just looking on not knowing exactly what to do. The amazing timing took us all on a journey together. Had it not been for my mom's dear friends' invitation, I would not have had this wonderful church family to surround and support me. After a couple of visits, I knew I wanted to be involved with this church. The Pastor was a remarkable individual that had lots of love to share. I was embraced not only by the church members but by the Pastor himself. He administers an amazing work in the community, in and out of the church, at home and abroad. He ministers daily to a host of people some of which are lonely, neglected and the under-privileged. After being introduced to the church, finding myself involved with ministry, it was approximately 2-3 months before Moms passing. There was just enough time for the church family to get to know me and to embrace me before mom's final roll call. I shed many tears up to this point, but nothing like this past Sunday.

I couldn't make sense of it until that day, when I realized that I was holding on with a "death grip" no pun intended. I held so tight, I was resisting what really happened consequently, I was in complete denial. It was as if I truly thought she was going to come back any minute. My body and spirit was so accustomed to her presence. I believe our spirits wil forever be connected. It is spiritual, not physical. It is the physical part that allows me to hear her voice or hold her hand. I still feel very connected spiritually but most of all, I won't be able to reach over and kiss her face.

"In the journey of life, we are associated with many beginnings and endings." -----*Marcia Lewis*

"You may shackle me in pain, you may call my name in vain, but you will not stop the angel's wings from lifting me higher." -----*Marcia Lewis*

<u>ON CRYING</u>

When I was but a wee girl, I took language at face value. I later learned that semantics can be very confusing. I completely understand how people from other countries can be confused with the English language. There are many languages which are much easier to understand than English. I found myself taking expressions to heart preceded by an emotional frenzy as they were completely misunderstood. My soul was in a quandary, when things did not seem right or when I lacked the understanding of something. I tried to understand anything that was communicated to me. As far back as I can recall I've always been that way. I am certain my friends can attest to that. It may be a bit annoying at times, but it works for me. I am reminded of the stories Mom would share with me about how I would not simply agree with anyone who tried to persuade me about something just because. I was a polite child, but I was not the agreeable type especially if I hadn't a clear understanding. Instead I would reply, "I'm sorry, I don't understand what you mean."

There was one particular song by OC Smith called, "Little Green Apples." Seeing how perplex little minds can be, the chorus stood out in my mind. The lyrics read, "God didn't make little green apples......" I stopped right there, thinking how could anyone say such a thing? The context of the song took me for a confusing spin. This saddened me greatly, to the point of tears. Here it is a famous singer talking about little apples that were not made by God? There was conflict with what I was taught in church; someone had surely lied to me. I had difficulty understanding all the facets of a God of the Universe that was not authentic if He was not the creator of ALL THINGS. I was told that it was only a song. That was not sufficient. Sacrilege was not an option. After getting insufficient "brush offs" and no real answers, I chose to keep it inside to analyze. I was tormented trying to figure it out for a few days. I took it seriously and I cried in silence because I thought it was my own issue when everyone else seemed to think it was okay. Well, it was poetry in song as I grew to realize later, but at the time I could not interpret it and in my eyes, there was something very wrong with this concept.

This taught me a great lesson in the end. When I finally decided to let it go, I grew from that experience through my tears. In fact, I later learned that crying is a very necessary thing to do. It helps to wash all the pain away. In fact, I believe it is a natural and healthy way to emote. A sure way to release the buildup of tension, frustration, sadness, anger, confusion is by way of one's tears. In addition, a multitude of other emotions that could potentially cause stress which could result in strokes, high blood pressure and other "diseases" if they are not released in some fashion. Emotions pinned up inside create stress in the body which result in unnecessary strife. After tears come, a metamorphosis of change begins resulting in relief, rebirth and reconnection. There are also feelings of joy, surprise, astonishment and spirituality that can bring one to tears as well. Tears of joy are tears all the same. I did my share of crying naturally as a young girl. I was a teenager before I realized that many considered crying to be a shameful thing. Many little boys were taught that they should not cry. My perception of crying was a very natural and normal display of emotion. Who said crying was for girls only? Someone told an untruth, because if that were the case, God would've given tear ducts to girls exclusively. Everyone was afforded tear ducts for obvious reasons. Many of us are taught to keep our emotions bottled deep inside or to be ashamed of things that are very natural occurrences. It is a personal, sacred thing that sometimes exposes ones innermost. That could be an intimidating factor for many.

The spirit needs a physical way to emote. Usually after a good cry one feels such a release that enables us to carry on in a direction that is clearer and often times more positive. Words can often get in the way of our true expressions when tears have the ability to replace all words at the onset. I learned that it is perfectly fine to cry in fact, it is good to cry. I used to cry in silence, but today I sometimes cannot contain it; perhaps it is not necessary to do so. There is no shame in crying as many of us have been taught to believe. I find myself apologizing when there is no need. Everyone cries at some time in their lives and if they don't, their feelings calcify and make them extremely difficult to be around. To cry is to liberate oneself from all the worlds' turmoil, which offers us the good and the bad. Tears are a necessary release. What a phenomenon it is to experience both joy and pain through crying. Like oceans, our tears wash away all of life's debris. Water moves in a path of least resistance and is often considered the path to wisdom. It is clearing, a purging. We all need a chance to start again and I can't think of a better way. Water is very sacred and should be treated as such; not some shameful thing we must hide. Referencing tears as a form of water from the eyes is represented symbolically by purification and fertility in some parts of the world.

Morning Sun

With the morning sun peeking through the crystal curtain meshed
with variegated billowy clouds as its background
peeking through generously, bright rays of sunshine.
Like God using His fingertips lighting the way for the promises the day
brings. The beauty of His mystery and certainty illuminates the path
that directs us with prominence and authority.
Remarkably infusing my soul with love and light that passes through
me as a conduit that is imparted to so many along the way—
Her Orange and blue hues radiate the vibrations of love in the
atmosphere—

-----*Marcia Lewis*

Chapter Seven
COMMON THREADS

So, on Sunday the most marvelous miracle made itself known in my presence; I was pleasured by witnessing it. It is fitting that I had a witness because I would have had the most difficult time trying to tell anyone what had taken place. One of my dear friends who I share a great deal in common with had been on my mind off and on all morning during church. We seem to understand each other through spiritual silence, through music and equally as well with words. We experienced together new heights of music exploration; all of this transpiring after 40 years of age. This makes for a unique and extremely special kind of relationship, thus having so many things in common.

On this particular Sunday morning between services, I was found in my usual place in the prayer room, playing piano. Worship time alone is very cathartic. I was working on some musical arrangements that she created for the poem I wrote for Mom the night she went to Heaven. I felt a tugging on the inside to call her as it had been a little while since we spoke. I continued to work on the music as I reminded myself that I would call before the day was over. After church, the telephone rang. The caller I.D. showed her name and I pleasantly thought how connected we really were. Excitedly answering I yelled out her name! "Guess who has been on my mind all morning," I exclaimed. The response was startling. Instead I hear someone say, "Hello???" in a bewildered, disoriented voice. Much to my dismay, I responded as perplexity set in, not knowing who this could be. Before I could ask, the stranger on the other end said that she had no idea how she got my number. Now, out of all the contacts my girlfriend has, how my name came up to call, will forever remain a mystery. I know it was only God that marvelously orchestrated this. As this miraculous picture began to unfold, I am convinced that the moment I had the urge to call her is the instant this person found the telephone. She was placed on my mind so that I might be prepared to help.

By this time, I am floored! I took the woman's number and got on the telephone to call my friend at home to deliver the good news. I was so happy to be the chosen one, the one that God entrusted to carry this mission through. I was equally pleased to know that I was chosen to be part of this unusual equation. She was on one end of California and I on the other. Hence, there are many people in the world who still have good intentions and are without malice. My friend could hardly believe this story. Our connectedness was clearly evident that this was orchestrated in the heavenly places. How on earth was I the one she called? The Master had it set up that way and sent the Holy Spirit to do His work. Incredible little stories like this let me know He is real. They are marvelous bits of Masterful hands working in the phenomenon that cannot be explained. His works are so powerful we cannot begin to understand. However, that is not our job. His thoughts and ways are higher than ours. They are simply by design, certainly not by coincidence. Everyone won't understand the significance of this and just lean towards the theory that this is just some kind of odd fluke. Pay attention! Listen and life will reveal itself to you. I have learned through years of experience to fully trust in the one who heals with love, protects and guides with His marvelous light and gently whispers His promises in our ears. If only we open our spiritual eyes to see and our ears to hear. No matter what belief one may have, it is evident that there is a power much greater than us that direct our paths. **OH GREAT HOLY SPIRIT!!**

Manifestations

As I drove along the coast the marine layer was thick. It made me stop to contemplate my life. I examined all that was flourishing and all that was not. I sought meaningful change in my life and help to understand how to move on without my beloved Mom. As Mothers' Day was approaching, I thought it was an appropriate time to readjust things in my head and in my Moms former dwelling which became mine. I talked to the Lord about it because I desired His perfect will to reign over my life. A dear elderly gentleman came into my life to consul me. He talked me through some difficult places in my mind and gave me the comfort of an uncle I never had. It was the perfect time to receive him into my life. Comfort came from the Lord first and then He sent some earthly help as well. He was kind and gentle as he shared with me some biblical scripture as well as good old-fashioned wisdom. God knows what we need far before we do and He places before us learning opportunities through life experiences while we are unaware of what He is doing. "Our job is simply to trust and obey and watch Him move in a miraculous way."

Meanwhile, the holiday weekend was most difficult. Staying busy helped to mask the pain, however, it doesn't disappear. Grief is incomplete. My thinking during this period was especially strange while desperately needing my Mom to talk to. I think she may have had a chat with the Master to manifest an earthly being on earth to help me with my particular state of mind. It worked, he came just in time.

"My first-born grandson radiates joy"

Angels

Circa December, 2017 I met a lady who was a traveling nurse coming to this part of town for the first time. She was a bit frustrated about the motel she was staying in. On special assignment, she mentioned how ideal it would be to have a room to rent during her temporary stay. Something beckoned me to tell this woman I had a place for rent. I had no fear about mentioning it to her until I realized that I had known this woman for approximately 10 minutes. It suddenly occurred to me that I may not want to tell her just that soon as she was virtually a stranger. I did tell her that I might know someone who might be able to accommodate her. We exchanged numbers and that was the end of the story for then. Being that I talked to people all the time, I let it pass without a second glance for the next couple of days. Maybe a week or so later, I happened to be reminded of this woman as I mentioned our first encounter to a loved one in passing. As I hung up the telephone, a passenger requested a ride and I made my way to the location. When I got closer to my destination, I recognized this familiar name but it was a common one so I didn't pay much attention. When I arrived to pick up this person, it was at the same location I picked up this woman before and the name was the same.

She steps out walking towards me and it was confirmed that after asking for a sign and speaking about her the same morning, I knew that she was meant be a brief breeze in the interwoven pieces of my life's fabric. She asked about the location and the specifics about who was letting the space. Prayerfully and oh so carefully, I told her that I was the one with the room. I told her the particulars and left it alone. I told her to give it some thought and I would be available to show the property to see if this would be a good fit for her. Soon enough she called and I had her over to have a look. She liked it, especially the green plants outdoors. We were prayerful about what potential roommates would look like. She prayed, I prayed and after a few weeks past, we were roommates. She fell in love with my outdoor plants. Upon arrival, she got out of the car and immediately started talking to my plants. I had neglected the poor plants and at the moment I realized just how much. I would sprinkle a little water once in a while as I travelled to and fro. Knowing how much mom loved the plants, I would water them as if I expected her to come back to water them herself. It was too painful, knowing it was her pride and joy. Even before she went away, the plants needed attention because she wasn't able to tend to them as she once did. Mom had the best neighbors of all time who stepped in to water them. They were starting to over grow in the pots and needed some real attention. Some roots were water-logged, overgrown and choked out. This woman stepped out of the car as if they had been waiting for her. I was stunned by her immediate attention yet pleasantly anticipating the outcome. This was my first official room-mate. More importantly, this was the first time sharing my bequeathed space with someone for more than a few nights, although we intended her stay to be a very short one. It allowed me to get out of the rut I was in. I was forced to remove some of my mom's belongings, (Not many however), and moving just a few of her things helped me deal with reality a bit more in her absence. I had to move out some things in order to make room for the new. After doing so, this lady moved in and helped to stir the energy around a bit for me. Prior to her moving with me, all I did was eat, breath, sleep and cry in my Mom's absence. All I could think of was her. My neighbor was so awesome. She was quick to help me make a change after Moms transition. I could hardly begin to do anything; I was numb. I was working very hard, staying extremely busy and crying during work at any given time day or night. My sweet neighbor, who affectionately calls me sissy, looked after me and encouraged me to make a change even when I didn't feel I was ready. She convinced me that I needed to make little transitions by painting some rooms. Change was positive and vehemently necessary in this cycle of my life. Through my hardest times, she was there. This helped in so many ways, I cannot begin to express.

I'd never seen someone with such a passion for indoor and outdoor house plants. She got busy with plans and free advice. She incurred the expense of buying larger planters, soil, nutrients for plants and started her project. She had the entire driveway filled with upside down plants with soil everywhere as she reconstructed my entire little outside garden. I thought that this could be a disaster as she left things undone for more than a few days. Something hushed my angst and made me still. I watched even though I wanted to intervene but I followed my instinct. When she was done, it was beautiful; both of us were pleased. She was ready to do more planting and arranging when she got the news that her assignment had been terminated. As quickly as I met her, she came and she went. A few days before Valentine's Day, I understood that she was sent for a designated time, who flew away to go home. She said she was coming back, but somehow, I knew that this astonishing presence had come for a specific purpose. It was as if my Mom sent her to come for a specific reason and when her job was done, so was she. It was astonishing to watch my Mom through this lady. I knew Mom would approve of her coming to help like she did. I am certain that angels are all around and they can be sent from a celestial place and somehow, I think that love can be silently manifested by the power thereof. I know that an Angel came, not by coincidence, to look over me in ways I could not at the time.

Damelo (Give it to me)

Just like Sunshine, smile and give me your heart
Every energy vibration is an integral part
You cannot keep it all to yourself; you must give it away;
Everyday
It can ultimately help you find your way
Just curve your mouth upwards on both sides and form your lips to say
"I'm alive"
In your gratitude say thanks and you will surely thrive
If you hide this practice deep inside,
You will then begin the start
To freely give of your heart

-----*Marcia Lewis*

Chapter 8
Le Joie de la vie

Beyond all of my expectations and all of my wildest imaginations, motherhood was the gift of all gifts. The first gift was particularly special because it was brand new. For God to grant this gift on the day before a holiday celebrated around the world was even more remarkable. My Prince was born the day before we celebrate the birth of the Prince of Peace. There was a song that happened to resonate in a special way after I gave birth to my first born, that explained this extraordinary feeling quite well. This song leapt into my spirit and sat down posing itself as my theme song. One of the major artists at that time released a song entitled, "Never Knew Love like This Before." This song at the time was a number one top seller on Billboard charts with frequent radio rotation. It would often come to my mind without thinking about it. The moment my baby looked into my eyes, I passionately recognized that there had to be life in him far beyond his years. It was perfectly apparent that he had been here many times before. I was enlightened by his presence. When I looked into his eyes, I said to him, "You've been here before." His beautiful brown eyes sparkled yes. The wisdom in his eyes revealed that of an old soul which left me speechless. Everything about the birth was completely natural. Long before my son was due, my plan was to do it "my way" wholeheartedly.

I wanted to give birth naturally without any assistance from medications to both of my children. Well, that part worked out fine. I also decided I would not conform to regular baby food; rather I would cook fresh food and blend it by hand at every meal being served. Perception is not always reality, however. Yes, I was determined he would wear cloth diapers as nothing else what be good enough to touch my babies skin. I planned to nurse him and administer to him a meatless diet. We would not practice pagan holidays, so I thought. .... "The true meaning of holidays are often hidden by inaccurate fables, myths and many other unnecessary stories," said I. Needless to say, every meal was not hand blended yet, his processed foods were very few and selectively chosen. The best "healthy start" I could give him was from me exclusively. The nutrients from mothers' milk are unparalleled. I hired a personal diaper service and that was actually set up in advance. My first experience with cloth diapers was hilarious. Being home after the first few weeks or more, I complained to my mom that the cloth diapers were not what I expected, as they seemed to have a shrinking quality. I am thinking that perhaps these diapers were not 100% cotton or something to that effect. I told my Mother about my concern and she hollered with laughter out loud! I was bewildered thinking what could be so funny? Here I am, trying to be a conscientious mother and I almost had my feelings hurt. After being so tickled, she lovingly responded. She said, "Honey, the diapers are not shrinking, the baby is growing!" At that point, we both laughed out loud even though I felt like a 27-year-old dunce trying to be all grown up and mature. That was my first lesson that proved I needed to consider that I didn't have it all together as I had hoped. Perception is not always reality. I apparently had many things to learn about motherhood. This brand-new experience had a huge learning curve, all the more marvelous. My love bundle was full of wisdom, growing much too fast and already putting me to the test. He had these mesmerizing eyes that could look directly through a person and then turn on this smile with two dimples in his cheeks. Women were drawn to him and I was forever being approached about commercial work or ads. The thing that was most unique about this little person was that he knew when to turn on his charm. Although photogenic was he, when you turned on a camera, he was more interested in the camera itself than posing for someone. He would instinctively know what your intentions were. Intentionally, he would not give you the time of day. As soon as the attention was directed elsewhere he would be back to himself with all his natural charm.

Enlightenment number one: As a brand-new mom you have no real time for yourself. It is all about the family and not so much about you. (This requires a superb balancing act; it can be done). Your baby knows more than you think they know. The things you do while pregnant have a direct effect on the child. I was in the recording studio most of my pregnancy and he has been poetically musical ever since, old "skool," but of course.

I was heavily influenced by the Rastafarian movement. During my residency in London, I learned the significance of belonging to a group that stood for Biblical practice that lent itself to dreading the ways of society; the Babylon system was inharmonious. Consequently, I named my babies middle names to reflect that ideology. The first born was named after Halie Selassi I, who reigned as the greatest emperor of Ethiopia and hailed as the earth born savior for Rastafarians. Hence the name, Tafari (he who inspires awe), was chosen for his second name. I later learned that Haile Selassi was my grandfather's favorite world leader. My second son was given the name King in Swahili, which is Rais. In Latin the word is rex, regis meaning the same. Names are very important. My hope was that their names will always precede them.

When my second Prince was born, we had a bit of a Code Blue emergency.

I thought everything was fine until my body shut down. I hadn't begun the dilating process even though I was having a few contractions and suddenly the umbilical cord was compromising our safety. Before I realized what was happening, the medical professionals were rushing me into the delivery room for an emergency C-section. There was no time to wait; only time to say a quick prayer which was enough. We had a safe journey in the delivery room and he was a healthy, bouncing baby boy. Gods' favor was evident in the midst from the very start. This little guy came into this atmosphere with many things to talk about already. In amazement, the moment he came home he wouldn't stop talking. I suppose due to the turbulence in the delivery process of his arrival, he had a few things to say about it. Both he and his brother had good dispositions and didn't cry unless they needed something. Adoringly, I whispered, "Why do you talk so much, already?" Here I was, just coming from the hospital after a tumultuous time, and he wouldn't let me have a minute to collect myself unless he was asleep, of course. He was a loving child who loved to be on the move. My precious little busy body. My father said that he would be a preacher. Fate hasn't shown us that yet, but he is definitely a communicator with a streak of good luck. At one point, we gave him the nickname, "Lucky." We never know what the future holds for us. When it was story time, every night before bed he would be delighted (Probably because it involved communication).

Lesson number two: In a busy world, it is best to be able to have some time at home with children away from work if possible. It is a labor-intensive job to juggle all the things to do in a days' time when you are working a regular 9 to 5. Organizing time to do many things at once was tiring. A highly respected yet underrated duty. READ TO THEM. No technology takes the place of reading and influencing them with music.

*****

Assuredly this was my child and he was going to make his presence known wherever he went. This I knew for sure, even when the occasion called for silence. By the time my second baby came into our lives I was sure of a few more things instinctively. Truly he has proven to be the live wire. He was also considered the "lucky one."

Enlightenment number two: fruit never falls far from the tree. I did not have time for many other activities outside motherhood because it was a full-time job and my world revolved around my boys. I taught them early on that "we are a trinity and in time, after I am long gone they will be the dynamic duo so always love each other. "Take care of yourselves collectively and separately because self-preservation is the first law of nature." I always wanted them to remain close and rely on one another as brothers.

I never found what I wanted in a mate for myself when they were young. I wanted someone who was kind, genuine, intelligent, relatively good looking, more like Prince Charming. Much to my dismay that person never came to be. Well, if they did come, they were already occupied in one way or another.

I did get close but no cigar. Well, at least not in America. Shortly after I had my first child, I believed I had met my "soul-mate" overseas but we were young and not ready to face life as an inter-racial couple at the time. Germany was brutal in ways that we were not willing to try to confront while the US had issues far worse in other ways. We could not see a clear path for raising two little brown boys in a society such as ours. It was enough for us to deal with when we were together, but the babies wouldn't understand and would be subjected to unnecessary lines of discrimination. Protection for my offspring was first priority and overruled anything for myself. Decision making for three was a huge responsibility yet, I knew that I didn't want to take the chance of risking their peace of mind for what I wanted. Although, I now realize that if Mommy doesn't have peace then the entire family suffers. That is another story entirely. I wanted a good man in their lives or none at all. I knew I was very capable and that I would have some explaining to do as they got older. I was ready for the challenge ahead as a single parent although I kept my eyes open for that special one along the way. Meanwhile, I had my duty to fully raise my children. God was on my side, and I felt like a supernatural individual that could handle all odds. I wanted very much to provide the ideal role model, but I made some poor choices. I found it difficult to juggle the different roles and find balance simultaneously. It was being a wife, being a mother, being a daughter, being an educator, an employee and seeking some kind of balance in my own life spiritually, mentally and physically. Not an easy task at all. I felt like I could have made some better fellow choices in retrospect, but I wanted my children at the same time and I gave them all I had to give. I believed that I could take on the challenge alone and do an excellent job with it. My guys needed to be here and I needed to be the mother with the fathers that made the contribution. My sons are so precious to me and if I hadn't mated with these guys I would never have had the opportunity of knowing, teaching and supporting these magnificent men that God chose me to parent, to love, guide and protect. Having said that, I did a lot of praying along the way because I knew how hard the road would be, but with the Masters help, we got by. Not only did we get by, we scored big time. These two men are wonderful individuals that have made a significant impression on people about who they are and what they stand for. I entered parenthood hopeful with a dream and vision for my two, to be great leaders in this life, with whatever they chose to do. I always told them to "be the best at being themselves which is more than I could hope for. You can speak your destiny into existence by the power of the tongue. Education does not only come from school alone, it comes from every direction. We can expand our intelligence without getting a PhD and become anything we wish with a steadfast mind, courage and fortitude to get the work done. It is important to love your family (not only blood), all over the world, no matter the color, creed or nation as we are all inter-related in some fashion."

Lesson three: Often time's people are less likely to stand by you in your own family than friends outside who stand closer than a brother.

My babies were well protected during their days before school. In fact, they were very sheltered. When it came time for them to face the real world, away from me and in school I taught them to stand up for themselves. Living in a place of love at home and having to face the cruelties of the real world was something I wasn't prepared for. "Be kind, but firm enough to defend yourself," I warned. "Always stand for what is right and by all means protect you. Don't start the fight, but be sure you finish and finish well." Although in an ideal world we would like to trust everyone, but this is not the case. Trust the Creator of this Universe and then your Mom. With God's help, we will make it. We prayed every day, together and individually.

I experienced being bullied as a youngster; I didn't want my babies to experience this as I did. I didn't allow toy guns of any sort in my home. I later learned that when you make something off limits, all they want to do is play with guns the moment they go to friends.

Once they started in school, practicing holiday traditions were all the rage for them. My hopes for doing it my way, living in our society as we did, quickly flew right out of the window! Santa Claus and the tooth fairy were prominent characters that I could not seem to get out of their minds, so I taught them the real meanings as best I could and explained as they got older that these fables come from traditional customs rather than real life. They understood as they grew older to appreciate both and not to believe every story they were told.

After a while, my kids were not buying the Santa story anyway, nor did I try to push the issue. When everyone around you is raving about Santa Claus and how many gifts were received, it is hard to tell your children otherwise in a manner that they will understand, until they are old enough to reason. I never was a fan when it came to boasting about material things. It was indeed a difficult balance. We played a few little incentive games, so that if you achieve well in school and practice good behavior, your gift requests will be fulfilled by the big guy as best as possible. Like everyone else I guess.

One time I tried to set a place for Santa to come through the night for a spot of "cookies and milk." Well, that was short lived I blew it in a big way. Having wrapped presents half the night, setting up Santa for a snack and after tending to their needs, I was exhausted! I slept right through getting up to remove the snack. Needless, to say when the children awakened and found that Santa hadn't eaten his cookies, the milk was rancid and yet the presents were neatly placed under the tree by the Chimney, something did not add up. Game over!

The "tooth fairy" idea came into play very well though; I took every advantage of using these times for an incentive plan. I was able to pull it off successfully for a number of years. I was proud that I was able to perform well enough to place money under their pillows without being discovered. I think I secretly got some kind of rush as I slyly made it in and out of the room unnoticed. I think I remember my eldest say he thought he saw her sneaking across the window seal. What fun we shared growing together through good and bad times. A great lesson I learned was that my world had to revolve around the love for my children. I had to over compensate for the lack of a father in place. I left myself out of the equation to see that their lives were as fulfilling as they could be under the circumstances. There were far more good times than not. I knew that I needed to keep positive role models in their sight. I could teach them many things, but I believe that there are some things a woman simply cannot exhibit quite like a man can. It needs to come from a man. Just in the nick of time, as the boys were entering their pre-teens, I met a wonderful man who became my life partner. He was monumental in all of our lives for many years. He was good to the boys as if they were his biological children and that is what we considered him to be: Dad. He is their dad to this day. In fact, we had three sons. His son's age was conveniently sandwiched between my youngest and oldest. They were stair steps about two years apart. We made a nice little package of love together. His guidance and love was unparalleled. He protected us from the start and I am ever grateful for the love he has shown us. As a result, they have a close relationship and that kind of unity, one cannot pay for. My Mom was an integral part of their upbringing; thank God for her undying love and guidance. My Aunt, (Moms oldest sister) took care of my first born as I was on the road, off and on, for the first year of his life. I was singing with extended family in the UK, *Soul II Soul,* that achieved great success in the music industry on an international level. In fact, I had embarked on my lifelong dream as a singer when I was delivered the best Christmas of all time, my first born. For the wondrous gifts that God made me responsible for, my sons, I would do it all again. They are my joy, my loves and there is nothing in this world as fine as Motherhood. There is something to be said for being responsible for human beings. These two had my DNA, but there are many who do not but the life lesson is the same. I've had three foster children for a short while, who taught me how difficult parenting can be. I believe, although challenging, Motherhood is the best title one can be awarded. One of my greatest lessons of parenting was that you can teach your children how to live but they must want it for themselves and it is ultimately their decision. We are placed here to give guidance and assistance. I learned that I cannot control their lives; I can only point them in the right direction by living my truth and by setting the best example possible. That was a hard lesson to learn. I thought I had full control, not so. Essentially, they must do it for themselves. If you raise a child in the way he must go he may or may not depart from it. Of course, every parent's prayer is to have their children successful in every way. There are other influences that can interfere, but with Gods good grace and mercy all things are possible. I pray that I've served my children well and that they will serve their children accordingly.

There have been trillions of books written over the years on how to parent, yet all the dynamics are different in every situation. There is no sure-fire way to do anything because what works for one may not work for another and vice versa.

Someone once said that we do the best we can with the knowledge and awareness that we have. I interpreted that as the old adage that I grew up hearing all the time. "In all your endeavors, be the very best you can be."

Angels come from every corner of the earth. It is our job to recognize them, cultivate and guide. My angel babies are flourishing in the world today. What a gift; the ultimate joys in my lifetime.

On Bullying

I felt like the only child growing up because my brother, my idol, my role model, my heartbeat was 15 years my senior. Needless to say, he was almost a grown up and it was quiet at home for me as a result until my baby brother was born. I was happy to be called his big sister I wore that title well. I am sure he will attest to that today. We were very close growing-up together and whenever we had an occasion to be away from one another, we were happy to see each other again. We would fuss all the time, but that was our mode of getting along as brother and sister. We protected one another so that no one else could talk to us like we did ourselves.

As much as my big brother was my hero, I so wanted him to come home from the Army to see me. I could think of my brother or ask about him and he would call or we'd receive a letter in the mail from him. It was the most special thing to know I had a big brother; I just wanted him to be in closer proximity. That was not possible, for he was already a young man.

Growing up as I did, I had to use a lot of imagination since I usually wound up playing in solitaire. When I was about seven, we moved to a community that was affectionately called Baldwin Hills and at the time it was a fairly decent area. It was a collective of glamorized apartment lifestyle living. Some places had beautiful panoramic views of Los Angeles. Today, it is referred to as the Jungle; hence, it is a different day. Moving to a new neighborhood meant going to another school and making new friends. I was excited about the new change. When I got to the school, I immediately drew attention from the teachers who noticed how different I was from all the others. Most of my teachers seemed to want me close to them as if to protect me. The children at this school were particularly interested in me, because I was the different girl, being new to the campus. Also, the fact that I didn't behave like the others drew more attention to the "new girl." I didn't quite dress the same, talk the same and being that I was rather shy, I did not talk very much to most class-mates. I had very few friends at this school. It was rather uncomfortable, to say the least. With peer pressure at its high, survival in this school became challenging. The more I tried to go unnoticed, the more noticed I became. Everyone seemed to get along smoothly in the little clicks at school and I felt like an outcast. Thankfully, I was quiet and well behaved, which looked good in my teachers' eyes. I was considered bright; consequently, they kept me close.

The boys thought I was interesting and cute, I guess. Maybe it was just interesting enough to chase me at school. The boys wanted to include me in games like, "Hide and go get it." It was terribly disturbing for me because I did not want to play. In fact, it was frightful. I had already been crying to my Mom about this terrible game they wanted to involve me in. She suggested that if this continued having talked to the teachers and staff about it, to take matters into my own hands. The day came when my mother's words to me rang in my head, which gave me the courage to stand up for myself.

One day we had a fire drill and I was the flag monitor that week which I considered a truly honorable status. My duties included bringing in the flag and being sure that all the balls were collected and safely returned to the coatroom in our class. As teachers pet by then, I took my job very seriously. The so-called king of the school decided that he liked me, I suppose, and plotted to trap me in the coat room knowing that I would be alone. Unbeknownst to me, this guy and his buddy came into the coat room to block me in. It was a dark hallway type closet that had openings on both ends. They were moving in from both sides and I felt like I was being smothered, trapped as they crept, attempting to close in on me. Somehow, that day, something in me was awakened. All of a sudden, I became this endangered species from the wild jungle, who heard my mother's voice. With nowhere to run, I kicked him so hard that he bent over shouting about his pain. His flunky friend went to see if he was okay as I ran for dear life! To this day, the thought makes me cringe knowing the fear that I faced that day. Word spread quickly that the quiet girl was to be left alone. My daddy said to me later in life that I would be a dangerous subject, if I was forced into a threatening situation. He believed that I could handle myself. Luckily, I haven't had many occasions to arise as such, but I don't think it would be too pretty.

Bullying is a coward's act. I feel very strongly about protecting others that are victimized by those who wish to inflict cruel acts towards others. When I hear of school-aged children who succumb to the pressures of being bullied, it breaks my heart. I have empathy for others in this position because I was bullied. It wasn't long before I learned to protect myself.

The only good thing that I've gleaned from these experiences is that I can stand up for myself and I am not afraid to raise my voice about injustices of any kind whatsoever. I prefer to fight on an intellectual level for what is right and just and fair. Perhaps I missed my calling; perhaps I should have been a lawyer as many friends have suggested.

I never believed that someone should have the right to try to control another person and their actions. I lived by the golden rule. Do unto others as you would have them do unto you. Mrs. Markham was my 6th grade teacher. We would have to recite these words as she stood for fairness and once again I was her pet. She was the first person in my life that exhibited the actions of a liberated woman. She rode a Harley to work most days, she was tall and statuesque and she was a boss who was always in charge in all directions. Everything she did seemed to make a statement, especially the way she walked. She was the director of all faculty meetings. Quite a phenomenal woman she was. When she walked in the room, she had a command that was unfounded. I was so proud of Mrs. Markham and I knew that she was proud of me. I believe she was my all- time favorite teacher. In fact, she would have me come into the room during recesses and lunch time so that I could help her grade papers. That was a privilege for me. As I look back, I wonder if she wasn't trying to protect me from the wolves outside. In any case, it created in me a desire to teach and I have been doing so in and out of the classroom ever since.

Chapter 9
Perception

The definition of perception by way of google explains it is a way of regarding, understanding, or interpreting something. After all this relatively strict upbringing, I was taught to believe in certain things. In many ways, my conditioning stemmed from generations of people of the same belief. My perception of these things was often slanted by my own naivety. I was guarded so much that when I got to real adult life, it was very different. It was not what I perceived it to be. I imagine there should be the perfect balance between exposure and protection when raising a child. Is there a perfect balance? That might be the ideal question. I think that I was so sheltered and protected that I missed some real-life moments of understanding about the way the world really works. But in time and in my own eyes I walk in the light now more than ever.

Real life begins for me at 50. Who knew? Embarking upon the second half of my life, I begin the dance by tapping into the unknown without fear; reaching the intangible inner spirit. Today, my inner spirit woman gets a voice. As a result, I've had my spiritual eye opened. I've stepped into a knowingness that no doctorate of philosophy (PhD) can compare with. I call it the enlightenment zone, my quiet place and space. This thing called life is interesting and most rewarding if you allow it to be. Life is never quite the same after these experiences. Somehow, we realize that some of the things we thought were important aren't really important at all. Life lessons build character and teach us the things we should learn to develop from. Hopefully, you too will find the essence of what truly matters.

*****

God has granted us the power to will a particular thing or idea into existence. It is customary to expect certain things to be a certain way according to the conditioning and experience. I have learned that it is not always a good idea. In fact, it is the opposite. If we commit things into the hands of the Man who walked on water, we realize that He didn't have to try to walk on the water, He simply did! I reflect upon this story and think about the ease in which He walked. I don't believe that He was examining His past experiences or even what He was taught. He had faith and walked knowing that His help was already in place.

So, when I was a teenager my upstairs buddy who eventually became one of my greatest friends of my lifetime, introduced me directly to entertainment. His dad was a musician who played the Vibes. As a young teenager, my mom trusted me with this neighborhood kid who was trusted and loved by my mom and everyone else as well. We soon became best buddies and we'd go most everywhere together. He made really good grades in school and would often help me with my homework as he was a few grade levels higher than I. I admired his witty conduct and his good ideas and intelligence. I had an extraordinary advantage of having the perks of a boyfriend without going on an official date or having an actual boyfriend as such. We explored daring situations and had a terrific time while doing so. We lived in a fantasy world of our own as we embarked upon teenage years. Most things no one thought was funny but the two of us. We were truly in our own crazy space. In the summer, we would explore with maps to movie stars homes; somehow, we found the courage to walk up to the doors of houses like Diana Ross, Smokey Robinson and Sammy Davis, Jr. We would go to the beach a lot and worship the sun for hours at a time using the most exotic sun tan lotions we could get our hands on. He would accompany me to a few concerts of my choice but due to his dads' connections, he often had tickets to all kinds of musical shows and premiere's. We met some famous people and created some wild memories of things most teens only dreamt of. I wasn't aware that I was being groomed for something I really knew nothing about. It was the wondrous world of entertainment! Some of my family members perceived the whole entertainment industry to be wicked. Entertainment was considered to be an unwritten taboo in the eyes of my Aunts! My concept was different. I believed that if your talent is far above average, being in the right place at the right time, knowing the right people plus working super hard as a childhood prodigy simultaneously, there was a 25% chance you might get recognized. Back in the day, you were required to have many talents, not just one, (i.e.., sing, dance, act, etc....). In addition, you had to work under all kinds of pressure should you be fortunate enough for opportunity to knock on your door. In other words, chances were extremely slim. I guess one could call it luck but I grew to lean towards the law of least effort along with positive thinking. At the time, I knew nothing of this law. All I knew is that I loved the whole sparkle dazzle affect and the whole notion of show business.

* * * * *

It didn't happen like that for me at all. Coming from a religious upbringing, entertainment was sort of unspoken, un- recognized as anything worthwhile! I was one of many children forced to sing in church. I am so happy that my Aunts jumped right in to help me out of my shell, because I was really timid.

This helped to eliminate a lot of stage fright. I guess this was the only singing they truly approved of. My Mom was always in my ear about being what I wanted as long as it was done with dignity and class. My curiosity grew and my imagination ran wild. I wanted to explore even more. My friend and I would sit for hours listening to lyrics as we dissected their meanings extensively. He exposed me to Yma Sumac who was one of the most famous proponents of exotica music of her time. How fascinating her voice was Ms. Sumac sang Peruvian music which led me to eye-opening wonders of world music and culture. I knew I had to be involved with music in some capacity that allowed me to see past teaching all the kids next door how to play in "Marcia's piano class." There had to be more I conceded. This class consisted of me playing the teacher, (of course) and everyone else participating in the class activities until everyone was bored out of their minds, save me. My pseudo classroom consisted of kids younger and older than I. Although I imagined myself in the lights, I had no idea that it would ever be more than singing in church which seemed to be quite enough for me, at the time.

Yes, he and I were in the age of experimentation and we were exposed to many things together. I began to take a few acting classes with my buddy just as a hobby and something fun to do as we were adventurous type kids. I can recall the concerts we went to, often times we would be allowed backstage which were nothing less than magical. My bud wanted to be an actor and I secretly wanted to be a singer.

Many concerts we would be allowed "all access" backstage passes and the glamour and fast pace thrilled me to a point of euphoria. My friend would always school me on 'how to look cool', as if it were no big deal hanging around all the big wigs. It was all I could do to contain myself. After so many of these events, I began to visualize myself singing with these entertainers on stage and actually starting to believe that I was in their place; actually, replacing them. As I developed my craft, I knew nothing about visualization at the time, yet I imagined myself doing the singers job. Not that my talent was even half as good as theirs, but I knew that it was an art form and mine could eventually contribute in some small way. I held on to that idea as I continued to explore music and theatre in church and around the house. Actually, any chance I got, I would sing to myself when no one was around. When pushed, I would sing to myself or I would sing with others only on special occasions.

My family members had a huge influence on me musically. My Dad sang in the back-porch basement with the Fifth Dimension as a needed baritone and bass. My Moms middle sister played her first gig at a Country Club where no blacks were allowed and continued to play throughout her lifetime. She was so fair in complexion; she was obviously light enough to get away with it.

My Aunt was a master at her craft; it came so naturally. She also played for church ever since I can remember. Their oldest sister played violin in local orchestral groups. My mom played in church for a short while until she was exposed to the hypocrisy in many churches. Although singing was inherent for me, all the hard work and dedication I really never had, yet I was surrounded by it which made a huge "impact" even still. What I had more of was a fantastic imagination!! All I knew is that some world-famous people were doing it and they were just like me except they had far more talent than I. I knew that my buddy couldn't help the process nor did I expect him to. Though, I often dreamed about what it might feel like, I had no idea I would travel the world with my voice one day. He certainly introduced me to it though. I was happy with backstage passes to get a glimpse of what life was like in this enchanting world of the stars.

*****

With a limited amount of experience, limited amount of natural talent and a boat load of enthusiasm, I took a giant leap one day. I went to England to visit my new-found friends that eventually became my English extended family.

*****

It was a dear friend of the family, who introduced us to begin with. She worked with my mom in one of the rare all black run hospitals in Los Angeles, where I was exposed to many famous folks in the community. I can still hear her fondly calling me "sweet girl." She was one that seemed to take a real interest in me. She always wanted to know what I was doing and she loved to expose me to the finer arts and culture. She was refined, charming and quite the intellectual type. She loved reading all kinds of literature. I suppose that was one of the many reasons they were friends. She had a house full of plants as she was a nature lover. Our birthdays were very close which made me feel especially close; I admired her a great deal. She believed in me as a person and saw something in me in the same way some of my favorite teachers did. I loved her in so many ways. She always had something interesting for me to ponder. After pondering she wanted a reply, an exchange. She was one of the ladies outside my family who truly wanted to hear from a girl who was raised in an era where children were to be seen and not always heard.

One day, she told my mom about a distant relative coming from England that she wanted us to meet. The expected guest was planning to bring her two children who happened to be our age and thought we would be a great match. So, we accompanied them to Disneyland and had a blast with our friends from abroad. It was fascinating to hear black people speaking the Queens' English.

The sister and I got along famously and told each other some deep dark secrets with which we vowed never to reveal to anyone and that sealed our friendship in that short period of time. We both liked to sing and stay up late sharing our most intimate experiences in our young lives. We had many things in common although we lived on opposite sides of the world.

My girlfriend left me with an open invitation to come to England anytime and I decided I should pay them a visit. I found a great fare and concluded that I would just start my adult life in England. So many great entertainers found their beginnings in the United Kingdom, so why not me?

I was received with warm embraces and exposure to lots of great music. At that time, my friend's brother had formed a DJ'ing posse for certain 'Blues' which were considered underground parties. They called themselves *Soul II Soul*. We were invited to a little hole in the wall makeshift recording studios with eggshell cartons on the walls for better, homemade acoustics. My bestie, sister friend and I were equally fascinated by this process as we both loved to sing and we were being exposed at the same time to some fascinating technology on a much broader scale. It was the first time we had access to a 16-track sound board—a huge leap from a simple tape recorder that we were accustomed to. So, we recorded some hooks that sounded like commercials about the group of fabulous DJs. (I wish we had access to those initial recordings; I'm sure they were hilarious!) We had the best time being silly together, as we fantasized about infinite possibilities. The lines for applying for citizenship were so long, at 19, if felt disparaging. I decided to go back to the drawing board at home. Besides, the weather consisted of rain everyday which was difficult to grow accustomed to, especially coming from sunny California.

Shortly after my arrival back to the States' side, I got an alert from across the seas that there was a radio DJ that heard our attempt to create a commercial and wanted to know how they could get in contact with us again. Well, having no means to travel back to the UK in a short period of time, I just imagined how wonderful it could have been and flattered myself by the recognition. A few years later, they informed me that they signed a record deal and I was elated for them. I never knew anyone who had a huge musical career manifest itself as such. I found new hope that this musical thing could be achieved. Meanwhile, I got a job at Delta Air Lines which allowed me to travel and see the world. At this point with music being my first love, travel was my second love. One day my "bestie," sister- cousin-girlfriend in England called me and said that they had access to a real recording studio. They were in a position to fly me over to work on putting an album together. I nearly dropped the telephone knowing that my dream could potentially come to life. There was one small dilemma. I had a huge decision to make. Should I stay with Delta? This would afford me a fabulous career in the travel industry with multiple opportunities for growth. I assumed this could be the "big prize" behind door number one, or should I sit safely behind a desk and wonder . . . what if? Well the rest is history. No contest, I went for it!

Ironically, I was expecting my first child and even though I wondered what life would be like with my child's father, I never completely saw it coming into view. So, I packed up my bags and off to London I flew with baby in tow (riding as a first-class passenger on the inside). Upon leaving Delta Air Lines, the big joke was that I was going to sign with a record label called Virgin records and at this point it was quite obvious to everyone that I was hardly a virgin. My only friends in England instantly became my family. This bond is a connection just as deep as the blood that runs through my veins, for life, for always. My first and only bestie girlfriend in the UK along with her family soon became my host family abroad. She later became the God Mother for my first-born son. They welcomed me and loved me like a family member from the Stateside. Actually, that is what we were to each other. Shortly after I arrived I was quickly ushered in and out of limousines to and from the recording studios, photo sessions, interviews, dance sets, etc. Immediate grooming was done for the big stage in its totality. While enduring quite the crazy busy schedule with belly ready to pop, it was exhilarating. Being pregnant and on the run that much took some doing, due to the hormones raging out of control, (and I do mean out of control) it was an outrageous journey. After my darling first born arrived, I knew it was time to become a full-on Mommy. I was so enamored with my little "Pepito." He was my world and nothing else mattered. I had no idea how I could keep up the pace. I tried for a bit carrying him with me to England and we hired a Nanny to assist on the road.

The truth is opportunity doesn't always avail itself according to your perception. It comes when it does and you have got to be ready or rock steady to meet the challenge. I could not have been more unprepared! I had some basic fundamentals in place yet, and not very many; more zeal than anything. Talking about trying to balance with hormones soaring, new baby in tow, working my career, trying to concentrate while nursing and quiet time and flying abroad every couple of months, was an arduous venture. In the last trimester of my pregnancy, we'd already been to the UK several times. Delta was good to us back in those days. My humble beginnings were in church singing solos and eventually my parents formed a little girl group with girls that I didn't particularly like very much. College afforded me some vocal recitals, voice-overs and piano 101, maybe a little theory and jazz vocal interpretation sprinkled in with bits of Theatre. Overall, it was a dream with the least amount of effort involved. Bits of grooming were sprinkled throughout my life to bring me to the world stage.

Our impressions, beliefs of what can be achieved as a result of the work we put in, can sometimes be deceptive. Granted you must have some talent in whatever your interest is, but you need to position yourself and believe so strongly that it comes into manifestation and yes be just as prepared for handling the success as the actual craft itself, while performing a balance act between all these things and more. That is the piece of the puzzle that many people miss. I now believe that occurrences or things can be willed into existence. It is the law of least effort; law of attraction. It is real and I can testify to that. From visiting the Universal Amphitheatre, visualizing myself in place of the entertainer, to seeing it manifest before my eyes is remarkable! Dreams do come true. I used to believe that singing in front of twenty thousand folks would be breathtakingly frightening, yet I found that singing amongst a few was far more frightening. The ones that are few can look down your throat at every possible turn; however, the sea of waving hands in a tremendous crowd can be most exhilarating and exhausting at the same time. Intimacy took on another meaning.

There were a lot of steps in between yes, but once I saw that believing is achieving, I never stopped believing and seeing myself in this place. I would still be involved on a professional level, but family was far too important to me. I've gone on to do a lot of projects. I've produced and directed children's plays in the Christian school system, directed choirs when these opportunities were directly dropped in my lap. God is miraculous and He will do exceedingly abundantly more than you could ever imagine. The primary work involved is to stay focused on the goal and to believe! He will do the rest if it is His will, it shall be done. His will shall be done in your life if only you believe. Don't ever stop believing, ever!!!

Lesson: Perception tells us one thing; reality often tells us something else. A way of conditioning to achieve is far more important. ANYTHING IS POSSIBLE with the least amount of effort. Belief is number one! Of course, belief alone is not enough. To line up your faith with your action equals excellence. Keep on believing. Belief is number one.

Chapter 10
Graduation Day Pianissimo

I am often asked if I play piano. Very softly, my response is always, "No, I simply play enough to give voice lessons." The truth is that I play in my "piano closet" for self-satisfaction. I understand the mechanics of piano and a bit of theory to put it all together, but to actually play for someone other than a few brief choruses is rather difficult. I have heard many of my college professors say that 10,000 hours of practice "is the measuring gage used" to master an instrument. I believe I have paid my dues and I have enough knowledge to execute properly. It takes courage, confidence and coordination. How well I execute is the question. I have always aspired to accompany myself on piano although, I never felt adequate enough. My Aunt was the best piano player I ever knew. She was graceful and gentle on the keys. She would play effortlessly and it was pure joy to be entertained by her.

One fine day, I was challenged by my Pastor to come out of my comfort zone. I was very uncomfortable with the confrontation and never had I been called to action like this before. Usually my excuse would be sufficient and the conversation would end. It was an incredible step to take. I was terrified and extremely uncomfortable. When I am challenged I will usually give it a try. The Praise Team leader was also a guitar player. I thought it would be special to debut as a duet together. My intention was to have him play with me as a cushion so that if I made a mistake it could be easily covered. I rehearsed the song the way it felt to me even though it was rather different compared to the original version. This collaboration was four entities combined, which consisted of his guitar, my piano and our two voices. The irony was that we rehearsed together for maybe 5 minutes at best. We never had an official rehearsal. As crazy as it seemed, I was determined to do this with God's help. On a beautiful day in May, I performed for the first time publicly on piano. I met the challenge and it was so awe inspiring for me that I could not contain myself. Afterwards, I was ready for more and more.

It is never too late to get things done, to try new things as I was fully grown when this happened to me. We never stop growing, learning and reaching if we so desire. Sometimes we have to jump even when we cannot see the bottom. It's not always easy, but the rewards of self-gratification and accomplishment are profound enough to change your life, at any age.

Daddy's Girl

I remember when my Dad taught me how to swim; He was so patient and kind. It was something I looked forward to. Our time together was always special as he made me his number one priority. He was the perfect teacher and I learned quickly to swim even though I clung to him and wasn't completely ready to let go of him as my crutch. He shared with me a great lesson in trust and courage.

It was a warm summers' day after school and work for us as we walked along the poolside. We were jubilant and enjoying our time together, when suddenly he dropped me into the pool. I suppose he was intending for this to be my graduation day. He had been teaching me for a while and all procrastination ceased that day. At this point, he was more confident that I could swim than I was. I wanted to hold on to him as my safe guard. Well, he obviously knew this and decided it was time for me to make my move. This was one of my greatest lessons. My Dad was fully dressed which indicated to me that courage was going to have to be my best friend and that I had to trust myself to stay afloat. From that day forward, I swam like a fish. Daddy told me later that he knew I was ready for the water. If he hadn't dropped me in the water that day so spontaneously, I would have hung on to him as long as I could. Just like life itself, we must receive a bit of tough love that may appear to be difficult but in the end, find a tremendous gift is waiting. This gift was life changing and it taught me that it takes courage to hold your breath and jump into a situation that would otherwise linger for much too long. I trusted my Dad fully and even though he was dressed, he would have jumped in after me if necessary. With no time to contemplate what to do, it was my natural born instinct to swim for survival without any help from anyone. It was a time to depend solely on myself. I was the proudest little girl all summer and consequently, I was far more confident than ever before. One reason was that I could swim with no help and most importantly because my Dad taught two great lessons: how to swim and how to be courageous in all things. It helped me build my character and to be unafraid of difficult challenges. He taught me that I could do whatever I set my mind to. He showed me what it takes to trust and depend on the best person for the job. "Me!"

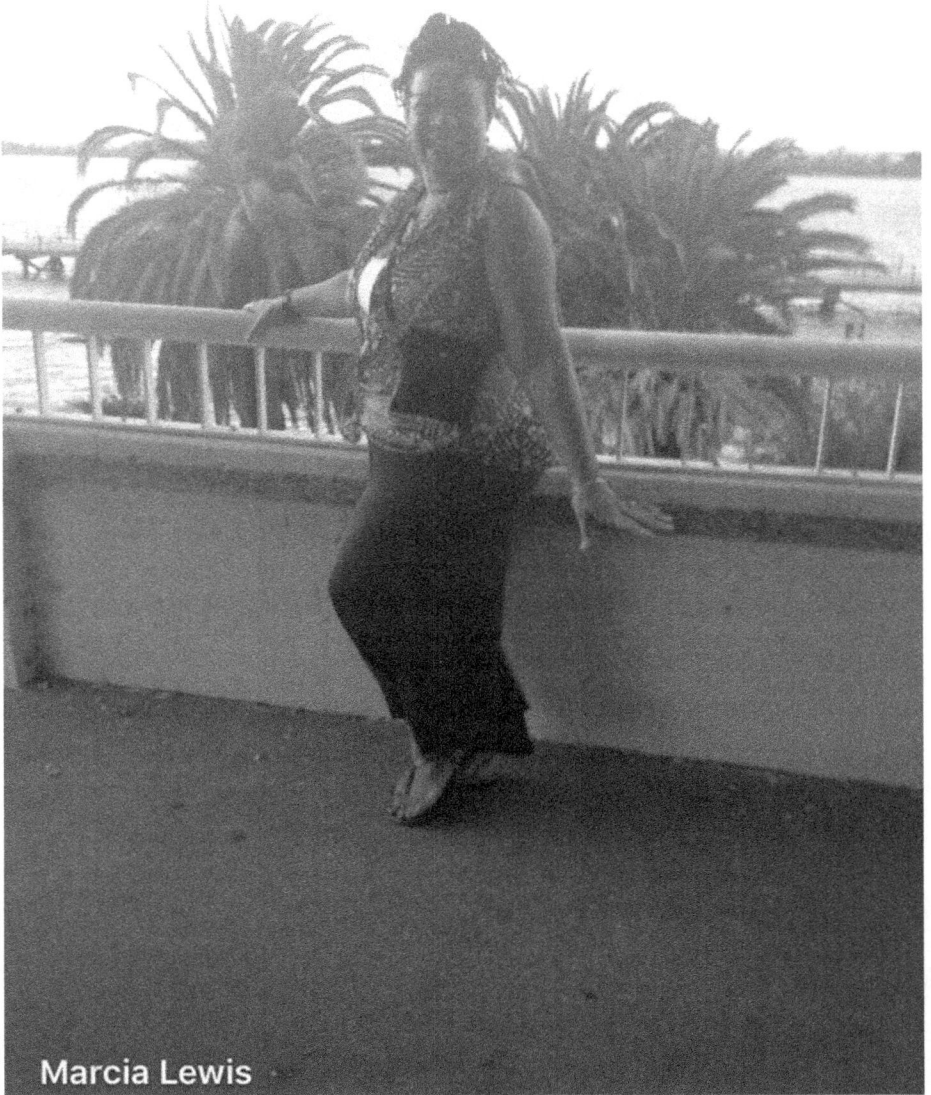

Marcia Lewis

Chapter 11
On Fear

The interesting thing about fear is that it is powerful enough to paralyze your body to the point that you cannot move, but at the very same time, it can make you realize the courage you never knew that you had. I once heard an acronym used that I thought very fitting: fight excuses and rise (FEAR). The fear of the unknown can cause a great amount of anxiety. Not long ago, there were a few mysterious men lurking around my dwelling without proper cause, rhyme or reason. One attempted to back his truck into my driveway; another claimed he was looking for his Mom after her long absence. My loving neighbor and friend stopped them each time. There were known burglaries in the neighborhood this season and suspected foul play was in the air. This troubled me quite a bit and I tried desperately to put it out of my mind. The thoughts of invasion kept lingering as there were three occasions in question for 3 weeks almost consecutively. What an eerie feeling to know someone is watching you or better still someone is trying to violate you. It was frightening to feel like someone was watching in hopes to take my possessions. Not that I have anything, I have nothing in the way of material. I was operating in fear and this fear came to create a snowball effect of fear that grew and grew and overcame me. It was this horrible feeling of vulnerability for there was nothing I could do. Suddenly I didn't want to go anywhere. It was more important for me to NOT leave as to guard my territory. Paranoia set in and before I knew it, I was feeling sorry for myself and for a moment in time, I was frozen with FEAR! I called my best friend who helped me snap out of it. He said to me, "Don't you dare stop. You must go ahead with your life and live it," as he shook me back into reality, thankfully. Fear is a demon that would like to devour you. In fact, it has tried too many times. I know what that looks like. This time it didn't work because I faced fear and it had to back down because it wasn't going to work on my psyche any more than it already had that day.

Fear is one of the things that will rob you of your positive energy if you are not cautious. Fear tries to change the navigation on our life compass and often times, for many of us, it is successful. Every problem that presents itself is a riddle we are faced with resolving. Fear is something that we must confront rather than retreat from, which is the easy alternative. Fear is not in and of itself, it is taught or believed. What I mean is we have been conditioned to embrace fear and therefore, give up. I am reminded of a brand-new baby seeing a giant size dog three times its size. Typically, the baby is not afraid unless the dog does something to alarm the little one. If we as adults act a certain way, then naturally the baby will react accordingly. Overcoming fear is necessary if the intent is to become courageous.

LETTING GO

There is this feeling I have had since my Moms transition that hasn't allowed me to fully let go of her. It is as if my heart hasn't caught up with what my mind already knows. I now live in her dwelling and everything has remained more or less the same as if I thought she was coming back. The pain was so deep that I could not face going through her belongings enough to move them from their original spot. In a way, I'd been paralyzed. With the exception of a very few items, to move them from the house was out of the question completely. Just the other day I learned a most valuable lesson. In fact, perhaps it was one of the best lessons I've ever been taught. The lesson is in letting go. Ironically, I often heard my mothers' voice say, "They are only material things, which can be replaced. They have very little value at all." That is very easy to say until you lose something or someone. Lessons are not always easily understood or accepted but when they come and you finally grasp the real meaning, you once again come back to the fact that nothing happens by coincidence, yet by design because there is a lesson to be learned in absolutely everything. It is a matter that requires us to be still and examine ourselves. How you perceive something on the exterior or physical self, is not always the interpretation from the inner spirit. We must be mindful enough to listen to the inner voice inside.

Walking around in partial grief and in partial contemplation about how I am to accept and adjust to life after my best friend has gone on to her resting place; I encountered a life changing incident. Trying to maintain my lifestyle, my sanity and my finances, I found a few oddly, scattered jobs which allowed me to at least tend to some of the bills that came up suddenly. As I started to embark on some of my other options, I was offered a temporary job in the management office at my complex. I was elated because this was something I had never done before yet, they were willing to have me in to assist while other permanent personnel were being placed. It was the pure favor from God. I asked and I received. I was obedient to His commands about certain things which afforded me the help I needed. Being in business for myself, my schedule is hectic and my movement is sometimes unpredictable. This one-week assignment changed my movement from erratic to steady instantly. The first day on the job, everyone was glad to see me there to help things run smoothly. Many congratulatory accolades were coming my way; everything seemed to be moving in the right direction. Being that my work was located on the premises there was no need to spend money for gas, I could run home for lunch and actually have time to sit for a while and get back to work all in a half hour of time. Never before has this happened so easily in just 30 minutes.

What a luxury this was for me. As I went to the house for my first 30-minute break, I entered as usual and I felt a presence in the house. I dismissed the thought when in fact there was no one there and everything looked somewhat the same as I left it. I happily ate lunch and skipped back to work feeling great. I worked the rest of the day and then proceeded to come home to change clothes and decided to work some hours on my second job feeling empowered, feeling hopeful that I would finally get a handle on some other bills that were overdue. Off to my second job I went and worked till later in the evening. Sensing a bit of accomplishment, I arrived back home to do some writing about how fabulous things were going in my life. I sat down at my computer to find an unusual breeze swirling around my neck. It was quite unusual and in fact rather haunting.

I looked over to my right and the vertical blinds were moving, yet there was no particular breeze outside that I was aware of. As I moved in closer, I realized I must have left the sliding glass door open but when the screen door was open also, assuredly something was very wrong. I had been burglarized? This feeling was one of sheer violation, rape, invasion and fear. It overtook me for a while. Yes, fear had its power over me at the onset. I ran outside to the neighbors and I found no one there. It was about 10 o'clock so I gathered my senses about me thinking that people around me could be asleep and how could I be so negligent. I came back in to check all the closets to make sure no one was hiding out.

Not sure what I would have done if anyone had been there, but all was clear and the odd thing was, I found everything was in its place as I could see. I called another neighbor who was just coming home; he rushed over and helped me to continue the search around the house. It was such a comfort to know that he was there for me simply for support. Mortified, terrified and rightly confused, my safety had been jeopardized. I looked around one last time and there was a drawer that was slightly ajar with a bright green sock peering at me in a most unusual way. I opened the drawer and bingo! They had very carefully searched through the drawers and found personal items in Moms jewelry box and mine. The burglars had the unmitigated gall to put everything back in its place. "Of all the nerve," I thought to myself. At a glance, I wanted to call my sons but that would alarm them and we would all be caught up in the moment of panic without any further resolution. It was already done. No need to upset everyone. Once I gathered my thought process a bit, I could not imagine being alone for the night in an unsafe place. That was my initial thought although, once I secured myself rigging up a miniscule contraption, the atmosphere changed enough that I felt semi-secure enough to sleep. By this time, it was about midnight and I managed to calm down enough to get my wits about me. I called the police to file a report. It all seemed to be very routine checks, and there were no fingerprints taken, just a warning to be careful and the report number he wrote on an ordinary little pocket-sized piece of lined paper. It was very unofficial. It was more like two fellas from the neighborhood coming to see that I was okay before going back to their homes to watch television. Completely overwhelmed, I drank some tea to help me to relax, imagining how I could possibly sleep after this. Eventually I did, as flabbergasted as I was. Anxiety haunted my every move as I felt like I was under 24-hour surveillance at every turn. Indeed, it was a fact. Living alone and having no one to watch over me felt desolate. Whoa it's me; poor me. I finally launched off to sleep hoping that when I awakened I would find that it was just some terrible nightmare and all would be back to normal.

The feeling I went to sleep with was not the feeling I awakened with. In fact, it was real and it was not a dream. It was so real I had to thank God as I always do, but this time, I offered special thanks. I was so grateful that no hurt, harm or danger came my way. The entire week dragged on with various emotions fluttering in and out of my mind and then the enormous lesson started to come. As grateful as I was to be out of harms' way I began to ponder Moms words. She would say, "What one dollar can buy, another dollar can replace." Her voice rings in my head often saying, "things are only things and that they do not define nor give credence to who a person is." It is essentially not important. Tears would build in my eyes thinking about how there were certain things that she held dear to her and other things that had a great sentimental value. I somehow wanted to protect that memory by having the jewels. Then I realized that I still have the memory! No one can ever take that away from me and that is what matters most. Sometimes the symbolic item is nice to have but "things" come and go every day. Our lives come and go the same way. How precious it is to have all the wonderful memories in my mind more than material items that can be replaced. Heirlooms are sentimental yes as we had quite a few, but the memory thereof, the sentiment is not tangible. Therefore, we always have everything we need. The presence of this woman and the impressions she made on my life are keepsakes far more than any heirloom.

One of my neighbors came to me with information that she felt was vital. It was a website that I could consult with to retrieve my things. I stopped her right there. There was no way I would consider buying back anything as it wasn't worth it to me. Earlier that day, I was thinking about how I had to let go and that I could not walk in fear. First of all, fear is not God-like. It creates anxiety, restlessness and an uneasiness that could fester and cause many "dis-eases." He taught us to be courageous while walking in His marvelous light, in alignment with truth, knowing that He would take care of all our needs according to His divine plan. Secondly, I realized I could no longer hold on to things that were no longer there. I had to let go of the idea that it was important to hang on to my Moms things that she would never come back to retrieve. Besides, I would not want to have anything that some criminal defiled by touching with dirty intentions. The thought made my stomach turn.

I told my sweet neighbor that I had decided earlier to move on because it was good for my mental health. It was not my job to chase criminals and that they would someday have to pay for it. My only hope was that someone would benefit from those things long after it left the criminals hands. I also derived from this experience that sometimes God has to teach us a lesson in letting go. I was hard headed because He urged me to let go of mom's things before and I gave away a few items.

Although it has been a year and a half, I felt like I was not ready. Well, He comes along in His majestic way and coaxes us into things that may seem at the onset to be something negative which then propels us into a new thing. This new thing that He wishes to show us is positioning us to understand what we must learn and how important it is to let go so that we can let God. Even if you are believer of Universal power and not necessarily a believer of Christian faith, you must know that we are here to earn life lessons from the Universe, which is a power far greater than us. I've studied the practice of letting go in all the areas of my life that had a hold on me. It is a learned practice.

Fear will hold us in a compromising position all our lives if we let it. So, with that being said, I derived a great lesson by being forced to let go of my moms' things, unhealthy thought patterns as well as unhealthy relationships. Trusting in only Him for His grace is sufficient for me. There was a relationship I was holding because it tied me to a connectedness when it may not have been the healthiest relationship. After this incident occurred in my life I was able to let go of many things. Many thoughts, sentiments, material things and hurtful words I was able to let go of. I started losing more weight. Things that were once so important lost some validity. It was a gentle reminder that we should not sweat the small stuff. Having my health, both physical as well as mental is so much more important than material things in life.

We don't need half of the material wealth that we have and the things that are most important are not tangible. Although it is a rather brutal way to receive a lesson, I totally get the moral of the story. The Lord Almighty knows what is good for us long before we do. It is a compelling way in which to get our attention, but as long as we learn the value in the story we've accomplished quite a bit. I shall not walk in fear; in fact, I will courageously move into a warrior position and be a spokesperson for the elderly people who are unable to fend for themselves as they once did. I want to be safe along with them. I will continue to be an advocate for them as long as I am able. To take advantage of the elderly is the worst thing imaginable. In honor of my Mom's memory, one of the best things I can do is fight for those who are unable to fight for themselves.

SILVER HAZE

When we parted ways in Sun City where we lived happily for a while, my Mom moved to Riverside and I to Sacramento. She decided to look into the Senior Home community. I had a time accepting the fact that she was a senior. In my eyes, she was a beauty super queen that would never grow old and I was not going to accept anything having to do with "seniorism." I suppose I was in utter denial. It didn't matter what I thought because it was ultimately her decision and I could only stand by with my feelings until I saw to it that she was happy. I came to see the place and thought, "well it is a nice community, but there were just too many old folks around." It gave me a haunting feeling as if it were a burial ground. In essence, it was exactly that for many. The lady that sold the house to her had lost her Mom in the unit she would be living in, which was way too much information for me. I wanted nothing to do with the place. I would visit her, but I made it clear that it wasn't my favorite. The peace came in knowing that she loved her home and the people around her. When I met some of her neighbors I realized that mom had found peace at last. After living with me and my noisy boys, she could finally do her thing exclusively without her children always banging around the place making unnecessary noise and headache for her. We had come to the end of our road living together. She needed her private adult life and so did I.

In parting, we said our "see you laters" and after I saw her all settled in, we journeyed onwards. There was a time of something like 13 years apart while mom gracefully grew older and more settled-in with her community. I suggested to her often during this time, that she should come to Sacramento to live with me and she said she would if there came a time when she could not manage on her own. When her health started to fail, she would not reveal it to me. I had to squeeze it out of her. She kept secrets from all her children, but especially me. Once she told me that it was her life and basically to buzz off. I was the one girl in the family who would often make a big stink over my mom because I was so concerned about all of her secret living. When I came to see her, she would put on her best face but something was clearly going on. She made my brother promise not to tell me when she was in the hospital until it was too late. When she got to a point that she could no longer look after herself, in her later years here on earth, I went to be by her side. I was working in the mental health field and had a decent income, but there was no question that I needed to place my life on pause, for hers. Little did I know that it was coming to a complete halt so soon, but she had been ill for longer than I knew. It was the most intimate time we ever had together. Our time was filled with prayer, passion, fear, tears of pain and agony, contemplation and love. Although we didn't talk about much preparation for the inevitable, we exchanged the bare necessities.

I remember getting here to go to the doctors' office with her. The doctor said it was a mandatory meeting needed with a family member. So, I came here from up North and attended this meeting only to find, there was nothing unusual taking place. In fact, it was a routine visit. At that very moment Mom and I had an epiphany simultaneously. It was a divine call for me to come to visit and we both understood that this visit was by design and not by coincidence. It was clearly evident that it was time for me to pack-up my things so that we could ride out the rest of our days together. This time, it would be without the children, it would be the two of us exclusively. It was our time. It was a time designated by the Master to say good-bye, to get closure. Looking back on that time it was the most precious time I ever spent with my mom. After moving in, I was certain that I would be able to nurse her back to health but it was much too late. The inevitable was ahead even though we dared to admit it. We both knew the end was drawing near. Today, I live in the place that I thought the very least of. The people here have rallied around me and my next-door neighbors have been my guardian angels who surrounded me with pure love. In fact, I never had neighbors this fabulous, ever!!! I am shining my brightest lights, growing and walking in the light and walking in her shadow: the silver haze.

"In that Silver Haze I hear Mom say, 'You are here for a bigger purpose. Not only to be with me, but a much bigger purpose. Wait and see.'

I encourage you to live for your bigger purpose, in the silver haze."
---*Marcia Lewis*

In Conclusion

I have observed and come to believe over the years that our lives were designed far before we reached planet mother earth. Envision a door, a luminous door far away in the distance that is waiting for you to open. This door is enticing you to get closer. The objective is to then find the path that leads to the door and once you get to it, then you must have the golden key to open it. At that point, one must step over the threshold where you've made it to the promised land. Sounds easy, right? Well, almost. Metaphorically speaking, the door represents what God has for us on the other side of the door waiting ever so patiently. The search symbolizes the time you spend with Him in humility and prayer. It is the precious time you take to seek His wise counsel on what must be done. Using the golden key represents the courage it takes to pick it up and then insert it into the lock that will open the door. Everything is set up for us already. It is a growing process that does not happen overnight. It is worth waiting for with patience and love. There is an abundant wealth waiting for us. It takes courage to walk in unforeseen territory. It takes faith to walk a path that is being led by someone else . . . actually a miracle, for there are no mistakes. When it is designed for you, you can move forward knowing that it is purposed by a source much greater than you. The time in quest could lead you to the door on a number of different roads which might have a few detours.

It takes a powerful connection to the door manufacturer who has the answer as to which road will provide the safest, most expedient travel. When you are connected to the source, and blind folded some parts of your journey, it will strengthen your walk of faith as you are ordered not to fear, but rather have faith that someone is guiding who knows the way. It becomes so much easier when you surrender to being led by this magnificent all knowing, all seeing power. As we open the door and step into the other side, you find there is pure light illuminating all that is around you. In that pure light, it's warm, it's enveloping you in its divinity. There will always be a few patchy clouds coming through, but at this point you've mastered the path through the labyrinth in your life and you've learned how to maneuver through difficult, tight spaces. You've also learned very well how to walk with blind folds on while divine direction prevails. You have learned to trust the still small voice. Recognition of that voice gets better and better the more connected you become. The timbre of that voice is undeniable. When being directed, focused and rooted in good soil, you suddenly realize that what you may have once considered a mistake is actually a miracle. Mistakes are simple teaching tools so that we learn a valuable lesson. However, if the lesson if not recognized as such, the lesson may continue until you've learned the value in the lesson and make the necessary corrections. It is not by coincidence it is by divine design.

In conclusion, be sure you seek your passion and persevere. It is necessary to get quiet and still so that all your mind chatter ceases. This mind chatter can be thought of as detours on your path. At least most of the chatter in your mind should cease, because it is the very thing that will distract you when you are not completely focused. Your path may not be a straight road, but it is a sure road. It is one designed by the Almighty. Whatever your faith, it is very necessary to seek counsel as we seek guidance from a higher source that is all knowing and all seeing so that you are sure to tread the right course.

You can be whatever you are designed to be. It is already available to you. You must walk in that which was made especially for you. One way you will know that you are on the right path is that the things that you set out to do will flow like water. It doesn't mean that conflict will not come, but in the end things will flow smoothly. When conflict comes, it is mandatory that you stay on your path, be consistent and most importantly believe. Don't let distractions through you off course. Even when things look rather dim and you don't know or see the outcome, you must know that it will work out according to the Master Plan. The Master Plan is always the best plan. We must surrender to a much greater power than ourselves. For me that Power is God. When things are too big for you to handle, you must come to the understanding that it is never too small for God. Know also that, "No Weapon Formed against You Shall Prosper", when in fact; you are working for the good of humankind.

In a world of little tolerance and even less patience, we must seek peace in the midst of any storm so that we can receive divine instruction. The peace will allow you to stay on the path that you were purposed for. Get still and ask the question, "What is it that You would have me to do?" Ask this with sincerity and earnestly apply it in all situations. He will answer your prayers and questions. I've learned that He doesn't always answer immediately. There is no shame in asking. Asking is a form of humility where pride has no place. If you don't get an answer immediately, it simply means wait. How many times have we asked a parent something and their response is not what you wish to hear or you are asked to give it time? It is the same difference. I ask you to invite the power larger than life to come in and reign in your life if you haven't done so already.

You were created for greatness and the world is waiting to hear from you. It is time to show up and be counted. Ask yourself this question. What will the world say about me when I'm gone? Did you cease the moment and live the best life possible? Did you serve others or did you wait to see what life served you? These are questions to ponder and if your answer is, I'm living the best life I know how and you are doing everything you can to contribute to those around you, well done. If there is more to be done in your life, then get to work!!!

I happen to believe that perception about things is not always reality. Often times, fear can stop your beginnings due to your unknown future, but if you continue to seek, you will find. You will find that most of the time, it is not at all what you thought, in fact, there is a better outcome than you may have imagined possible.

Everything that happens is by design according to the Master. It has very little to do with you. It is more important that we walk in the light that is already placed before us. You are like an actor in a theatre and you are the star of your own life. Nothing is by coincidence. Never give up on what you know you must do.

There is always more for me to do, yet sometimes it feels like I've just begun. Hence, life is just a moment. My life's work will never stop until my last breath. Then, I am sure there will be work of another kind to do. At the end of the day, I pray that my Maker will say that I've done well according to His judgment. I want to spread as much love as I can. I invite you to do the same. With patience and understanding and unshakeable faith anything is possible. If, while waiting for your answer, you are not sure what to do, start by encouraging people. You will find that as you encourage others, you encourage yourself. Encouragement then becomes a snowball effect while you watch and wait for miraculous results. Before you know it, you will be fulfilling part of your purpose. You see, we all need each other for no man can stand alone.

By all means say thank you. Be thankful for what you have been given thus far. Gratitude will not allow you to dwell on what could have been, for it is simply a waste of time. Be conscious of the wondrous miracles that have occurred in your life. What you have is far more relevant than the things that you don't. Concentrate on positive things so that anything less than that can be dispelled. Some may have to search deep to find positivity due to layers of pain and anguish, but I guarantee there is good that lies beneath. I completely understand how life can weigh you down. It's all in how you chose to perceive it. Strife does not have to be your reality. If you change the way you think about things, you will see brighter lights of hope and joy and resilience.

I've started a Facebook page called *Call Miss Marcy* which started as a forum for a talk show. Initially, I started filming in a television studio that eventually folded before I could submit it to the cable network. I stopped, pondered, wondered what would come to be. I decided to change the format so that this could be a place for people to share dialogue. This is a place to share thoughts, exchange ideas and create dialogue. You can submit questions about life lessons and experiences that you would like to discuss, exchange ideas and hopefully grow from. We all want to be heard and with tolerance and respect we can share in another point of view. I will give you feedback that will hopefully leave insight or at least something more to think about. It is a safe place where we can dialogue that may be helpful not only to you, but to others as well. Sharing your thoughts with others is cathartic and you never know how someone else's experience can uplift and brighten your day. I encourage you to take care of your health which includes three components: physical, mental and spiritual. As you govern what goes into your body for physical health it is also vital that you are aware of the products used on skin and hair. There are so many chemicals in products today that are unhealthy for us and we are not always aware of their detriment. I will introduce some of the natural products that I've created for a healthy body glow. These items are made with love and great care. I will also advertise for events that may be of interest to others.

I want to encourage you to be the best you can be and live life in abundance at whatever stage you may be in. I wish you love, success, and most of all light to walk in your unique path.

Be careful to shine your love light always.

Marcia Lewis

A Special thanks to Mr. Fleming:

There are some people that come into your life who are designed to love you unconditionally in your most desperate time of need. This is the case for my dear Mr. Fleming. He exhibited the role of a paternal uncle I'd never met. The truth is, he came into my life like a guardian to protect me and clothe me with words of wisdom. The warmth of his gentle smile, the coolness of his demeanor transcended time. Mr. Fleming came bearing many gifts. He brought with him the eminence of our ancestors. He brought education that cannot be absorbed from a book. He is a natural born orator, teacher, father but most of all I am honored to call him my friend. Mr. Fleming I thank you from the bottom to the top for allowing me to share a small portion of your great legacy in this body of work.

You may contact Mr. Fleming at CS@Facsn.com This email address was valid at time of publishing of this book, *By Design.*

All of Mr. Fleming's work in this book was used by permission.

"Always love"